GET OUT FOR GOOD

A PRACTICAL BIBLICAL GUIDE
FOR RELEASED PRISONERS
AND THEIR FAMILIES

SCOTT K. STROUD

We love to hear from our readers!
Please contact us at www.scottkstroud.com
with any questions, comments or suggestions.

Get Out for Good – Scott K. Stroud
Copyright © 2020

All rights reserved. No part of this publication may be reproduced, distributed, or transmitted in any form or by any means, including photocopying, recording, or other electronic or mechanical methods, without the prior written permission of the publisher, except in the case of brief quotations embodied in critical reviews and certain other noncommercial uses permitted by copyright law. For permission requests, write to the publisher, addressed "Attention: Permissions Coordinator," at the address below.

Unless otherwise indicated, Scripture quotations are taken from the Holy Bible, English Standard Version® (ESV®) Copyright © 2001 by Crossway Publishing, Wheaton, Illinois 60187, U.S.A.

ISBN: 979-8-60670108-7 (Paperback)

Cover design by Damonza
Editing and formatting by Kim Burger

Printed in the United States of America

First printing edition 2020

Published by Cornerstone Books
7335 Valle Pacifico Road
Salinas, CA 93907

RELIGION / Christian Life / Prison Ministry

www.scottkstroud.com

DEDICATED TO

Pete Lundin, Phil Haugen, Tom Parrish,
and Rick Knapp;
spiritual fathers who made all the difference.

INSPIRED BY

Angel and Christina from *Born this Way;*
your perseverance in the face of overwhelming
challenges motivated me to get writing.

THANKS TO

My Lord and Savior, Jesus Christ;
why you continue to use this "cracked vessel" is
beyond comprehension.

Book Sponsorship Program

Men and women in prison have limited access to the resources they need to ensure a successful transition to life on the outside.

Your tax-deductible donation can help them *Get Out for Good*. For only $10 per book, you can supply chaplains with this much-needed guide. Each chapter addresses a practical area most ex-offenders face.

Would you prayerfully consider giving hope to those without hope?

Contact us directly to hear about opportunities available to you or your church. Every dime goes toward our non-profit ministry and gets books directly into the hands of prisoners. Click on the sponsorship page at **www.scottkstroud.com** or email us at **sixstrouds@gmail.com.**

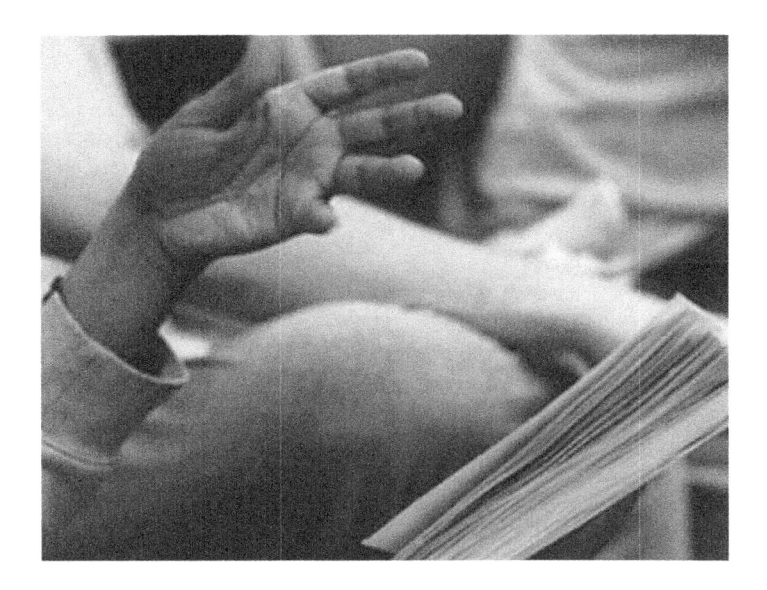

CONTENTS

Introduction 1
Part I: Relationship Basics 5
   CHAPTER 1—Get Right with God 7
   CHAPTER 2—Find a Mentor 19
   CHAPTER 3—Make Some Friends 31
   CHAPTER 4—Beware Romantic Relationships 45
PART II: Spiritual Growth 59
   CHAPTER 5—Take it Slow 61
   CHAPTER 6—Join a Good Church 73
   CHAPTER 7—Acquire Accountability 87
   CHAPTER 8—Do Your Devotions 101
PART III: Life Skills 115
   CHAPTER 9—Get a Job 117
   CHAPTER 10—Buy a House 131
   CHAPTER 11—Have Some Fun 145
PART IV: Leaving a Legacy 159
   CHAPTER 12—Become a Pillar in Society 161
   CHAPTER 13—When You Fall, Get Back Up 175
   CHAPTER 14—Give Back 189
   CHAPTER 15—Finish Strong 205
Afterword 219
Endnotes 223
Appendix 225
About the Author 227

Introduction
a typical story

I can't shake the memory of the sound of that steel jail door slamming behind me, locking me in my cell for the first time. It was August 16, 1990, the first time I heard that jarring noise, and the echo resounds through my nightmares to this day. As I slumped onto the bed in the holding cell, the adrenaline pumping through my veins from the high-speed chase I had just had with the Bloomington, Minnesota police department lingered. Earlier that morning, I awoke with a mild hangover and one thought: *I need money, and I need it fast!*

Since childhood, I had always been a thief, shoplifting whenever I could. I took change from our landlord's parked car. I walked into a house on my paper route and stole money off of the owner's nightstand (No one locked their home in rural Wisconsin). As a busboy, I helped myself to portions of the waitress's tips. I robbed the register at the department store where I sold shoes. I pinched a car from a restaurant by convincing the valet I lost my ticket but the car was mine. The list goes on and on.

But this time was going to be different. I needed instant cash. I was getting ready to move into an apartment with my girlfriend, and I didn't have my half of the rent since I had blown it on drinking at the clubs over the weekend. My brilliant plan was to get a fake gun and rob the cashier at a local restaurant.

So, I took a shower, dressed up in a suit, and slicked back my hair. I drove the stolen car to a nearby toy store and shoplifted my weapon, a convincing-looking black toy pistol. I picked out my target—a local diner bustling with breakfast customers—and then parked out front. I walked into the restaurant, past the counter, and straight into the restroom. I stood at the sink, for what seemed like an eternity, just staring at my face in the mirror. Tears began to form in my eyes. *What was I doing? Who had I become? Whatever happened to the bright kid with the infectious smile who loved to sing in school musicals and earned straight As?*

Just then, another guy walked in to use the restroom. I washed my face, took a deep breath, and walked out the door straight to the cashier's counter where a teenage girl was ringing up a customer. When it was my turn, I smiled at her and spoke softly. I was the "compassionate robber." I opened my suit jacket and showed her the toy gun tucked behind my belt. Her eyes widened, but then her training kicked in.

I had worked in many restaurants, so I knew the procedure for a robbery. The first step was to stay calm and give the guy what he wanted so a customer did not get shot. I handed the young cashier a paper bag and she put all the cash in it, a whopping $189. I grabbed the bag and quickly exited the diner. The restaurant manager must not have been there the day they talked about robbery procedures because he came running out of the front door screaming just as I got into my getaway car. I hit the gas and sped off, but he got the make, color, and license plate number of the vehicle before I made my escape.

One thing I learned that day was you can't outrun a police radio. I was on my way to attempt another robbery when a black and white spotted me. I tried to nonchalantly hide in a parking lot behind some apartment buildings, but within minutes five squad cars sped around the corner and surrounded my car. I hit the gas and cut across someone's back yard, trying to get away, but it had rained the night before, and my tires got stuck in the soft lawn.

With guns drawn, the officers closed in on my vehicle. My heart was pounding as they dragged me out of the car and onto the ground. They kept yelling, "Where's the gun?"

I cried out, "It's a toy! Don't shoot me!"

As they cuffed me and threw me in the back seat of the squad car, the realization that all my sins had caught up to me came crashing down on my shoulders. At age twenty-one, I figured my life was pretty much over.

The story of my arrest could be retold with slight differences by thousands of inmates across the globe, unfortunate circumstances leading to bad choices and ending in incarceration. Currently, there are over 2.3 million people behind bars in the United States alone. According to a report issued by the Sentencing Project, 1 out of 9 of those convicts are serving a life sentence.[i] That means, at some point, the remaining 8 will reenter society. But what happens to these individuals upon release? Do they learn their lesson and go on to lead a productive life? The statistics are sobering. National recidivism studies show that just over 75% will re-offend and end up back in the system within five years.[ii]

Thankfully, I was able to beat the odds. It has been 26 years and counting from the day my mom picked me up outside the prison gate upon completion of my four-year sentence. But my success didn't come by accident. Many factors came into play, which is how this book came about.

I believe if someone is willing to take the advice on the following pages to heart and begin to apply them in their daily decisions, not only can they stay out of jail but they can also go on to live the kind of life that Jesus spoke of when he said, "I have come that they might have life, and have it abundantly" (John 10:10).

Are you ready for an abundant life? Then it's time to get out for good!

Scott Stroud
Salinas, California

Part I
Relationship Basics

Get Right with God

"For the mind that is set on the flesh is hostile to God,
for it does not submit to God's Law; indeed, it cannot."
Romans 8:7

"Amazing grace, how sweet the sound
that saved a wretch like me."
John Newton

The judge's words caused murmurs of excitement to ripple through the small group of supporters who had come to stand by me at my sentencing. "Scott, I have reviewed the psychological assessment from the District Attorney's office, and I have concluded that you are not a hardened criminal. That's why I am giving you a chance to go to treatment instead of prison."

I glanced back at my grandpa and grandma, who both gave me hopeful smiles. The judge continued, "It's not going to be easy, but if you can complete the behavioral modification program at Nexus, we will drop the felony charges and stay your sentence."

My spirit soared! No prison? No felony record? Although I didn't know anything about the program, I was determined to complete it even if it killed me.

My first day at Nexus was a significant wake-up call. A group of about 25 men ranging in age from 18 to 30 gathered for group therapy. Now, I knew a thing or two about treatment. Growing up, my mom had some major social and emotional issues that tended to spill over into our family life. There were screaming matches with my step-dad at midnight, wild mood swings, and terrible rage-filled outbursts that usually resulted in nasty bruises up and down the back of my thighs. The positive side was she knew she was a mess and felt ashamed and guilty for her lack of control; thus, she sought help from professional therapists referred to her through Social Services. Considering I sat in on many "family sessions," I knew the right words to say to make the therapists nod, smile sympathetically, and write things in their yellow-lined notebooks. These experiences made me think that Nexus was going to be a cinch.

The confrontational therapy that was all the rage in the early 90s caught me off guard. A resident was singled out by the group for some small infraction. Then the entire group, including the staff, began yelling at him. "WHAT MAKES YOU THINK YOU HAVE THE RIGHT TO EAT TOM'S CANDY BAR?" The poor chap spent the next hour digging up his entire past to try to figure out what kind of personal defect would cause him to do such an outrageous thing. The first time I witnessed all of this, it took every ounce of self-control I had in me to keep from bursting out laughing.

The reason I wanted to laugh was that it all reminded me of my time in boot camp for the Army. The drill sergeants would yell the craziest things to try to rile us up. "STROUD! WHAT'S

GET OUT FOR GOOD

THAT HOLE IN YOUR EAR? DO YOU LIKE TO WEAR EARRINGS LIKE A GIRL?" The way I survived boot camp was the same way I planned on surviving Nexus—by keeping my head down and doing whatever anyone told me. I would use my wits and sheer willpower.

The Problem of Willpower

Human willpower has accomplished some amazing things in the history of humanity. The Great Wall of China, the Pyramids, and the Tower of Babel are just a few examples of what people can do when they put their minds to a task. But when you try to use sheer willpower to fix your mental and emotional problems, you quickly find that you run into a stone wall. I ran into this wall in my ninth month at Nexus.

The staff and residents decoded my strategy of ducking and dodging my deeply buried issues. The group increasingly targeted me for the afternoon scream sessions. All along, I knew the solution wasn't a psychological solution; instead, it was a spiritual one.

> The solution wasn't psychological; instead it was spiritual.

When I was a kid, we moved 27 times. Relocation was my mom's favorite go-to whenever her most recent relationship began to sour. During those times, she had learned to turn to local congregations for help. So, growing up, I was exposed multiple times to the Gospel message. I sat through Methodist Sunday school, went to Baptist camps, was confirmed in the Lutheran Church, and attended Pentecostal revival meetings.

The main problem was that whenever my mom decided it was time to move back in with my step-dad, we would quit going to church. This pattern taught me two things; first, the church was mostly for women, and second, it was only necessary in times of crisis. During my teen years, my family's Sunday attendance was very sporadic, and the lack of spiritual influence was evident in my increasingly rebellious behavior. I knew I was the prodigal son, but frankly, I didn't care.

At Nexus, all that began to change. I found the therapeutic approach wasn't working for me because all the messages I had heard as a child created a longing in my heart to be reunited with my Heavenly Father. The Holy Spirit was pursuing me and, after ten months of treatment, I decided to leave the program and have my sentence executed. I was relieved to be headed to prison to do my time. At least there I had a set goal, a date when I would get out rather than the uncertainty of wondering if I could complete the open-ended Nexus program.

Christ, the Cornerstone

In prison, I had the chance to attend barber school, and as part of our training, we cut the inmates' hair. Some Christian guys began witnessing to me regularly. I think they got together to strategize about who would be the next one to make an appointment with me so they could confront me with my need for salvation and forgiveness.

During that time, I moved into a different cell block known as the Honor House. It was the area of the prison for guys working hard to stay out of trouble while they served their sentence. I had heard about one of the inmates in that cell block who was convicted of a notorious crime. His name was David Brom, and at the age of 16, he killed his parents and his two younger siblings with an ax. I was curious about what kind of monster could do such a thing.

One day I saw some Christian guys I knew standing around Brom's cell door, so I wandered over to join the conversation. David was sitting on his bed and when he saw me, he smiled and waved me in. He was not what I had expected. He was 21 at the time, with shoulder-length straight blonde hair and a joyful way about him that made me confused.

How could a guy who had perpetrated such evil and was never getting out of prison be so peaceful?

All the guys in his cell were discussing a passage of Scripture, so I listened until it was time for evening lockdown. I lay on my bunk that night thinking about all the terrible things I had done in my life. I knew the Lord was calling me home.

About a week later, I was back in David's cell, and we were discussing Romans nine. Verse 20 stood out among all the others as it states, "But who are you, O man, to answer back to God? Will what is molded say to its molder, 'Why have you made me like this?'" All my life, I had wondered why God dealt me such a lousy hand. Why couldn't I have been born into a good Christian family like many of the kids I had met in church? At that moment, God spoke clearly through that verse. He said, "Scott, I placed you in your family for a reason. I was there with you from the very beginning. You can either continue to be mad at me, or you can follow me and see what I have in store for your life."

That night I knelt by my bedside and asked God to forgive me for all the sin in my life. I cried out to him, begging him to give me the kind of peace I saw in David Brom's life. Instantly, I felt a literal weight lift off of me! I knew God had forgiven me and everything was going to be all right. The prodigal son had returned home.

How's Your Foundation?

Jesus told a parable in Matthew 7:24-27 about two men who decided to build houses for themselves. One of them foolishly built his house on the sand. When the storm arrived, his home came crashing down because its foundation was not firm. The wise man built his house on bedrock. When the rains came, it stood firm because its foundation was solid. If you try to build your new life on the outside on the wrong kind of foundation, it's going to crumble.

The first step in staying out of prison for good is to build your life on Christ, the cornerstone. Any treatment program, rehab center, or half-way house that doesn't recognize this is only going to be able to offer you worldly methods based on popular psychology. The verse at the beginning of this chapter, Romans 8:7, shows us that the flesh, our sinful nature, is hostile to God; it cannot obey God's laws. Many have tried, and many have failed.

> **Build your new life on Christ, the cornerstone.**

However, just as I did, you might be thinking, *I can't return to my Father. He's too angry at me to ever let me back into the family. I've committed too many terrible sins.* The parable of the prodigal son makes it clear to us how God feels about lost souls. In Luke 15:20, Jesus says, "And he [the prodigal son] arose and came to his father. But while he was still a long way off, his father saw him and felt compassion, and ran and embraced him and kissed him."

My oldest son, Peter, moved away from home and took a position at a Christian retreat center about an hour from our house. One day, I was out in the yard working with my back to the street. At one point from behind me I heard, "Hey, Dad!" I was so surprised how emotional I became when I recognized his voice and realized he was home for a surprise visit.

Imagine the father's joy in this parable. This story was before texting, Skype, phone calls, or even a reliable mail service. It's evident he hasn't heard from his son in a long time. In the story, it almost seems like whenever the father is outside working, he finds himself glancing down the road to see if his son might be approaching. His longing was perhaps the reason why he saw him a long way off. His heart yearned for his son's return, which was why he took off running to greet him on the road as soon as he saw him. Does this seem like an angry father to you? Likewise, your Heavenly Father longs for your return.

Jesus said the way to destruction is broad, and many are on that way, but the way is narrow that leads to eternal life, and few find it. That narrow road is the only one that leads you back to your loving Father. Isn't it time you came home?

Heart Change vs. Behavioral Modification

There are three main goals that the penal system in the United States desires to achieve. First, it protects its citizens from criminals by securing them in prisons and jails. Secondly, it ensures that these convicts pay their debt to society by serving their sentence. Lastly, it works to modify the criminal's behavior so he or she might become a productive citizen after reentering society. In theory, the penal system accomplishes this third goal through education, vocational training, and outside volunteer groups that offer a variety of programs.

Changing someone's behavior is a worthy goal, but the Bible makes it clear that changing the actions of a man without addressing the issues of his heart is only a temporary fix, as his heart condition overflows into his entire life. In Luke 6:45, Jesus said, "The good person out of the good treasure of his heart produces good, and the evil person out of his evil treasure produces evil, for out of the abundance of the heart his mouth speaks." External pressures like the threat of punishment or confrontational therapy might make a person think twice about recommitting their crime. But, eventually, the wickedness of their heart will leak out all over their new life on the outside.

That is why the Scriptures speak so much about a man's need for a new heart. My second-born son, Elijah, was born with a defective heart valve. This genetic weakness made his heart susceptible to something called endocarditis, which is an infection of the tissue that makes up the valve. When he was 17, he got sick. We thought it was just the flu, but we kept an eye on him knowing these kinds of illnesses, which healthy people can fight off easily, could affect his defective valve. After about a week, he wasn't getting any better, so we decided to take him to the emergency room.

The doctors began to run some tests on him and quickly realized things were dire for Elijah; in fact, they were life-threatening. The doctors started to communicate with the children's heart clinic up at Stanford. Within an hour, he was in an ambulance on his way to Palo Alto. After two months of testing, they determined his defective valve had been damaged beyond recovery and scheduled him for a heart valve replacement. The titanium valve they surgically placed in his heart saved his life.

Your spiritual heart is defective from birth. It needs replacing if you are going to attempt to live a godly life. In Ezekiel 36:26, God makes a significant promise regarding this need. "And I will give you a new heart and a new spirit I will put within you. I will remove the heart of stone from your flesh and give you a new heart of flesh." Even though Elijah has a brand-new heart valve, that doesn't mean he will never struggle with health issues. It just means he now has the ability to lead a normal life.

Moreover, even with your new heart from the Lord, you will still face struggles. The big difference is now you have the power and ability to resist sin and make good choices because God's Spirit is inside of you, helping you every day. The Holy Spirit convicts you when you have fallen short, he comforts you when you feel guilty over a commandment you have broken, and he teaches you about God's holiness. Your behaviors will begin to align with his plans because good things will spill out into your life from a new spiritual heart.

Tips for Family and Friends

Tip #1 – Set a Good Example by Renewing Your Commitment to the Lord

I have met many people through the years who have high hopes for their son, daughter, or friend getting out of jail to lead a godly, productive life on the outside. They are happy the ex-offender has found God as their "solution to the problem." They may have even taken them to church when they were young thinking it was the right thing to do, but they have not continued in the faith themselves. They feel that Christianity is only for those who are "bad people" or are in crisis.

However, what's good for the goose is also good for the gander. The best thing you can do to help the newly-released prisoner on their new path of faith is to join them on that path. In that way, you will begin to share common ground, and get excited about their passions. Discuss the Bible together and seek to understand their joys and struggles concerning the Christian life.

When I got out of prison, many in my family recommitted their lives to Christ because they saw the genuine transformation taking place in my life. Recognize how the change taking place in their life is not just an accident, or because they have "learned their lesson." It's because of the incredible transformative power of the Holy Spirit working mightily in a new heart. You need that new heart just as much as they do, even though you might not have committed the kind of crimes they did.

Tip #2 – Don't Expect Your Loved One to Follow Your Exact Christian Path

Perhaps you are currently attending a church in a particular denomination that you love such as Baptist, Lutheran, or Catholic. You feel the best thing your child or friend could do is follow your path by joining your church or denomination. You must realize that in prison, chapel exposes the inmate to many different brands of Christianity. That is because multiple groups come in to hold Bible studies and teach classes on Christian living. Your denomination might not be one of those groups, and even if it is, your loved one might not have experienced the most significant impact from that particular group.

Let them pick their path. I have found that throughout my life, I have discovered influential Christians in every denomination. Now, that doesn't mean certain denominations don't have more doctrinal issues than others (See Chapter 6). It just means for the time being, the people that may have the most influence for good on the inmate might not fit your idea of the ideal spiritual guide. As long as the group they choose is dependable on the basics, hold your opinion to yourself and see what God does. You may end up squashing their newfound faith if you criticize the means by which it came to life.

Tip #3 – Give Them Room to Grow

Just because your child or friend has become a Christian doesn't mean he or she is not going to make some mistakes upon their release. They will face many struggles that you will have a hard time understanding. The main thing you can do is to encourage their reasonable efforts. Praise them when you see them making good choices and hold your tongue when you see them stumble a bit. If they have had a true conversion, God will complete his work in them. Remember the words of Philippians 1:6, "And I am sure of this, that he who began a good work in you will bring it to completion at the day of Jesus Christ."

Questions for Discussion

1. One of Scott's big hang-ups that prevented him from wanting to give his life to God was the perception that God had dealt him a lousy hand. What are some of the hang-ups in your life that are preventing you from coming to Christ?

2. God used Romans 9:20 to bring Scott to a place of decision. What are some of the Scripture passages that God is currently speaking to you through?

3. Scott found that confrontational therapy did not work for him because it didn't address his real spiritual needs. What are some things you have tried in the past that have failed to bring about real transformation?

4. God used Christian inmates to bring the Gospel message to Scott. What is God using in your life right now to bring his Good News to you?

5. What are some of your primary concerns regarding your family as you think about getting out?

6. What is the current level of spirituality in your family and among your closest friends?

7. If you have already placed your trust in Jesus for the salvation of your soul, talk about some of the things that have changed in you as a result of your new heart.

Find a Mentor

"For though you have countless guides in Christ,
you do not have many fathers. For I became your father in
Christ Jesus through the gospel."
1 Corinthians 4:15

"If I have seen further,
it is by standing on the shoulders of giants."
Sir Isaac Newton

My dad left my mom when I was four years old. I don't remember him well, just a vague shadow of a presence that never seemed to settle anywhere. The person that shaped and molded me into the man I was to become was female. I have to give her credit, though; she made a valiant effort at trying to be both mom and dad to me and my younger brother and sister. But I knew something was terribly wrong with this. I yearned for a dad. I saw other kids with their fathers and I was insanely jealous of them.

At the same time, I was scared of men. Not being around them much caused me to look at them suspiciously. I was worried the men who came into my mother's life were going to wreck our little family. I dreaded their heavy work boots, bearded faces, and deep voices. This strange combination of an intense desire to have a dad coupled with a palpable fear of men created much confusion for me in my formative years. As a result, I tried too hard when attempting to make friends, a tactic that caused boys to shun me, or worse, target me for bullying.

Eventually, I retreated to an inner life of fantasy, devouring fiction books in hopes of finding some connection with the characters I'd discovered there. My brother, Brett, who should have been my chief companion and confidant, became the main competition for my mother's affection instead. We constantly battled; screaming, scratching, and pounding on one another until red-hot tears burst free. I still have scars on my face today from those fights.

When I was in third grade, my mom remarried, but that didn't turn out to be the answer to all my hopes and prayers. Charles Langel was the twelfth of thirteen kids, raised in rural Wisconsin on a small dairy farm. I think my mom fell in love with him mainly because she was addicted to "Little House on the Prairie" and had a movie-star crush on Michael Landon. My step-dad, even though he had a similar name and looked a lot like the father on the show, was no Charles Ingalls.

Granted, he was a hardworking man and tried his best to provide for eight kids; three from my mom's first marriage, three from his first marriage, and two of their own. The main problem was all he did was work. He rarely talked to us; he didn't come to our sporting events or concerts. He didn't play with us or take us on family vacations, not even to a movie together. Most days, I wondered if he even knew we existed, except as additional labor for all the chores that needed doing for us to survive. On top of all this, he had no stomach for church, mainly because it interfered with work.

Although I do not blame my parents for the decisions I made that led to my incarceration, the lack of an active father in my life was a contributing factor to the brokenness I faced growing up. Most of the men I have ministered to in prisons over the last 26 years have had similar stories. I'm almost surprised when I meet a guy in prison that came from a well-functioning two-parent home. Absent fathers can have a significant negative impact on the lives of young men, but in the Lord, that doesn't have to be the end of their story.

> Absent fathers have a significant negative impact on young men.

Spiritual Fathers

As my prison sentence was nearing its end, I transferred to a medium-security prison in Lino Lakes, Minnesota. I began attending a Wednesday night Bible study where I met a man named Pete Lundin, who took an immediate interest in me and my Christian development. The week before I got out, he pulled me aside and gave me his phone number. "Give me a call when you get out."

Once I was released, I settled in at my grandparents' house where I was going to stay until I got back on my feet. That was when I decided to dig out Pete's number. We arranged to meet at Perkins for breakfast. We caught up for a bit, and I told him about some of the struggles I was already facing being back on the outside. He looked right at me and spoke the words that changed the direction of my life forever. He said, "Scott, you have a decision to make. You can be a good Christian, attend a local church, marry a nice Christian girl, and your life will probably turn out fine. Or you can be a disciple."

Emotion overcame me as tears filled my eyes. I knew I wanted the latter more than anything but I didn't know how to go about it. When I was in prison, the rigid structure framing my daily activities helped me stay on track. Outside of those walls, I felt overwhelmed by the freedom and temptation that seemed to be at every turn.

Pete went on to throw some real skin into the game. "My wife, Sandy, and I would like to invite you to come live with us. If you are willing, I would like to help guide you through the process of becoming a genuine man-of-God." He was offering to become my spiritual father.

A few weeks later, I moved into their finished basement in North Minneapolis. I began to witness first-hand what it meant to be a Christian husband, church leader, and, even though Pete and Sandy had no children of their own, they taught me how to be a good parent by treating me like a son, even though I was 25 years old. I ate meals with them, we went to church meetings together, I helped Pete with projects he was doing around the house, and we had countless conversations late into the night about the challenges I was going through. The impact they had on my life transformed me completely, so much so that I even named my first son after Pete.

You might look at the circumstances that led to this fantastic mentorship opportunity and think, *Scott got lucky. That can't happen to me. People like that are rare, and even if they exist, they probably won't take me in.* But I'm here to tell you that there are plenty of mentors out there; people who have a heart to see ex-cons get back on their feet and live a productive life on the outside. I have met them! Even though they might not fit the exact specifications of my story, there are spiritual mentors in every city around the United States.

While I wrote this book to assist prisoners and their families, I know there are many out there that will read these words and, just like the Lundins, have a heart for men and women that have been dealt a bad hand in life. There are many people who long to see these individuals experience a healthy family environment. I encourage you to go forth in the power of the Lord, and take that step toward fulfilling the ministry he has placed in your heart. Yes, it will be difficult. Pete and Sandy sacrificed a lot for me. There were nights Pete would stay up until midnight talking with me even though he had to get up the next morning at 5:30 to teach at the local high school. Amazingly, Sandy didn't even know me before I moved in. She just knew God's hand was in all of this, and she trusted her husband's judgment.

To my fellow ex-offender brothers and sisters out there, none of this happens by chance. You need to desire this kind of relationship with all that is within you. You need to begin to pray that the Lord will send you your own Pete and Sandy, but you also need to be willing to submit yourself to their guidance. In other words, you need to become a child all over again. You will have to relearn everything to dispel the negative ways of doing things that got you into your mess in the first place. To have spiritual parents, you will have to become a spiritual baby, recognizing that you don't know very much about living a healthy life in the real world.

Humility can be a big challenge for most prisoners, especially if they have been a Christian in prison for a long time. They feel like they have learned a lot about the Bible, and maybe they have. They have attended countless Bible studies and chapel services, worked their way through twelve-step programs, and become leaders among their inmate peers, perhaps even leading others to Christ. But the reality is they don't know the first thing about living as a Christian on the outside.

This lack of knowledge makes me think of James 4:10, which states, "Humble yourselves before the Lord, and he will exalt you." It's humbling to admit you don't know how to do essential things like maintain a healthy romantic relationship, hold a job, or be a good neighbor. It's when we confess we are lacking that we have the chance of being lifted in life and can achieve success in these crucial areas.

Where to Look

As my story shows, you can't just expect a mentor to seek you out while laying on your bunk in your cell. You need to begin to make connections with different ministries that are filled with men and women who desire to help make a difference in the lives of inmates. There are three main places I've seen fellow Christian prisoners find spiritual fathers and/or mothers: Bible study groups, outside ministries, and local congregations.

Prison Bible Studies

These groups seem like the most natural place to begin a mentoring process, because most Christians yearning to lead a Bible study already have a good grasp of the Scriptures and feel confident in explaining them to a new believer. However, it doesn't mean every person leading one of these studies is an excellent candidate to become your spiritual mentor. There are many reasons people get involved with prison ministry, and some of these motives can be a bit disconcerting.

In my experience, I have seen well-intended followers of Christ get involved with prison ministry only to be baffled by the inmates' complex questions and issues. Barely having answers for their own problems, they become quickly overwhelmed by the barrage of doctrinal arguments thrown at them. Others I've observed had what psychologists have called a Superman complex, feeling it was their mission in life to save people. The main problem with that issue is they cannot save the prisoner—only the Holy Spirit has that power as he works through the gifts distributed to the Body of Christ.

I have also seen a sad lack of spiritual maturity and gifting among those who would volunteer for prison ministry. These folks have tried their hand at other ministries in their church or parachurch organizations and have failed miserably. As a last resort, they try their hand at prison ministry, believing inmates are desperate for anyone to help them, yet that statement couldn't be further from the truth. My perception is it takes the finest and best to do prison work. It is not for the faint of heart, mainly because one will deal with some pretty major spiritual strongholds. Satan chuckles when he sees some ill-prepared, soft-kneed, Bible illiterate fellow strolling through the main gate thinking he is going to do these poor, unfortunate souls some good. On the contrary, he will be fortunate to walk out unscathed and with his faith intact.

> There's a sad lack of spiritual maturity among prison volunteers.

That being said, there are many Pete Lundins out there who not only possess a heart for the prisoner but also the maturity and courage to ride out the storm when the waves of life begin to crash over the side of the convict's boat. Attend as many Bible studies hosted by outside groups as you can, as you never know where you might find your mentor. As you seek out one, pray earnestly for the Lord to show you who he has selected for you. If you find someone you are naturally drawn to, begin to spend time talking with the person before and after the group. Help him or her get to know you and see if the Lord fosters a deeper, more meaningful relationship between the two of you.

Outside Ministries

Once you get out of prison, you will find that almost every church has a ministry for men and women. The types of events they hold range from weekly prayer breakfasts to monthly events. At the very least, most will have a ministry director with whom you can meet privately. These groups are excellent ways to begin to seek out a mentor on the outside since most of these men and women already have a heart to see young Christians gain a good understanding of the Bible and to apply these godly principles to their lives. Attend a couple of their events to get an idea of how deep or shallow the group is because not all ministries are created equal. Some may be like a social club for people to get together for fun activities like playing basketball, visiting local coffee shops, or going to the rifle range, while others are intent on discipleship, which is the very thing you are seeking.

Once you have determined that the men's or women's ministry is the kind you are looking for, don't overwhelm them with your need. Announcing to the group that you were just released from prison and are looking for a personal mentor is not the direction to take. Instead, ease into the group by showing you are interested in the overall health of every man or woman there; be the first to volunteer when menial chores need to get done, like washing the dishes after the prayer breakfast. If they have a service day to get some projects done around the church, be one of the first to arrive and last to leave so the group doesn't get the impression you are only there to leech off of them. Working together is how Christians build relationships.

Also, don't assume that the individual leading the group is the most natural one to be your mentor. He or she might be the alpha male or stand out like an Amazon woman, but their gifting may be administration and direction, not personal counseling. Take note of the people who show a genuine interest in your story and offer practical advice about everyday things like housing, job skills, and relationships. And whatever you do, don't ask if you can move into their house. Wait for them to offer. Remember, most people in the real world have a healthy skepticism about those getting out of jail—they don't want anyone to sucker them, and as the protector of the house their main job is the security of their family. Over time, they will begin to trust you and welcome you into more and more aspects of their lives.

Pastors of Local Congregations

As a pastor of a local congregation, I can tell you that ministry life is hectic. Ministers are involved in virtually every part of the operation of the church. There are countless meetings to attend, sermon preparation, Bible studies, shut-in and hospital visits, dinners with congregation members, and oversight of the property. Even so, most pastors have a huge heart for seeing people set free from bondage and will go out of their way to spend time with those who show a genuine interest in being disciples of Christ. Helping others is why they became ministers in the first place!

Once you determine which church you are going to make your home (I will discuss this in chapter six), call the office and set up an appointment to meet with the pastor for coffee or lunch. Be flexible and work with their schedule because it might take a couple of weeks to find a suitable time. At this initial meeting, tell the pastor your story and share your desire for mentorship. Your transparency will be appreciated and not an overwhelming request; in fact, it will probably be expected. There's a good chance the pastor will give you advice about getting involved with some of the groups offered by the church; follow through with attending these gatherings to show the pastor you are serious about discipleship.

Remember, when most pastors think of mentoring they think of programming. Pastors incorporate events into the congregation's life that are designed to impact the highest number of people. Their main focus will not be on personal one-on-one sessions, but rather group ones. Don't let this deter you! If they see you show interest in their suggestions, they will be more than willing to meet with you individually. At first, make it your goal to try to meet with the pastor once a month, but don't expect them to be the one to set up the meeting. Persistently call the office manager/secretary, also known as the gatekeeper, and see if you can squeeze into the schedule. Keep your sessions with the pastor to about an hour, not expecting all your issues to be solved in one sitting.

Tips for Family and Friends

Tip #1 – Avoid Jealousy

Everyone has a basic need for both natural parents and spiritual parents to be involved in their lives. As their natural parent, you may have been able to provide your child with spiritual guidance, but that direction can only take them so far. In fact, at some point in their journey, they might not be able to receive instruction from you because they feel it is just dad and mom telling them the same old thing they have been saying since they were a kid. Remember, they need a fresh voice to speak into their destiny.

That reality can be hard to swallow for parents. Parents can become jealous of the fact their child's mentor, who might be expressing some of the same ideologies as them, has a more prominent place in their child's life than the parents do. This conjures up feelings of replacement, even causing the parents to try to undermine the advice given by minimizing its impact or questioning its authenticity. Unless you suspect the mentor is giving false information or is going to harm your child in some way, try to hold your opinion to yourself and just let things unfold naturally. When they begin to exude some nugget of truth offered to them by their spiritual father or mother, don't retaliate by saying, "I've been telling you that for years and now you're finally getting it?" All this will do is force your child to decide between the parents they love and the new mentor they have found.

Tip #2 – When at all Possible, Get to Know the Mentor

I was very fortunate that my family embraced the Lundins and made them a part of our extended family. My family was glad when I moved into their home and they invited the Lundins to family gatherings, which allowed them to see me through the stories my family told about my past. My natural family and spiritual family worked together with a common goal—to provide me with all the help I needed to succeed on the outside.

Questions for Discussion

1. Pete Lundin challenged Scott by asking him if he wanted to be a 'nice' Christian or a disciple. What do you think is the difference?

2. What are some of the activities you are currently involved with that might provide opportunities for you to develop a relationship with a potential future mentor?

3. Scott talked about three places you can turn to when seeking a mentor. Which of these three (prison Bible studies, outside ministries, pastors) appeals to you the most? Why?

4. What are some of the reasons you need parental relationships beyond your natural father or mother?

5. How do you think your family and friends will react to you being 'adopted' by spiritual parents?

6. If you begin to sense jealousy in your natural family concerning your new relationship with a mentor, what are some things you can do to address their feelings?

7. Try to think of some examples in Scripture of relationships between spiritual fathers and sons (mothers and daughters). What impact did those mentors have on the ones being discipled?

Make Some Friends

"Iron sharpens iron, and one man sharpens another."
Proverbs 27:17

"Friendship is born at that moment when one person says to another, 'What! You too? I thought I was the only one.'"
C. S. Lewis

Brian and Mark took a significant risk when they decided to visit me in prison based solely on the recommendation of a friend. About two months before my release, a young woman named Lizabeth came into Minnesota's Lino Lakes medium-security corrections facility with a community singing group to perform for the inmates. After the concert, the performers had a chance to chat with the guys; she and I spent about 15 minutes talking. Lizabeth, in a moment of revelation from the Lord, recognized I was going to need a group of peers to surround and support me when I got out. She told Brian and Mark about me, and we met for the first time in the prison visiting room about a week later.

Within days of our first visit, Brian and Mark began planning my 'Getting Out of the Slammer Party.' They invited everyone they could think of to celebrate with this ex-con they had never met. Thus began what became known as the Kinship Group. We would meet for times of worship, try out new restaurants, and go on outings together. It was with this group of friends that I spent the majority of the three years following my discharge from incarceration. I was never bored because of the laughter, joy, and tears that filled my days as we celebrated one another's victories and mourned one another's defeats.

Shortly after my release, Brian moved in with me to share Pete and Sandy Lundin's basement. One day at church during testimony time, a guy named Jeff got up and shared about his renewed faith. I was sitting with Brian and Mark, and we all looked at each other with the same thought—this guy needed to be part of our group. From that point on, the four of us were inseparable. God knew I needed these three guys in my life to help me make a healthy transition to the outside world.

Breaking Free from the "Old Gang"

The dictionary defines providence as the protective care of God. Seemingly chance events, like how Lizabeth singled me out after the prison concert, are God's providential hand caring for us through random encounters. Being naturally introverted, God knew he would have to proactively work to ensure that friends surrounded me during the crucial transitional months and years ahead. Being a loner before I went to prison, I never dreamed I would find such amazing friends as the ones I discovered in the Kinship Group.

On the flip side of the coin, you may end up having an entirely different problem. Perhaps before your incarceration you were a natural extrovert and surrounded yourself with a group of friends who supported and encouraged you in your criminal way of living. You might even have been a member of an actual, recognized gang like the Crips, Bloods, Aryan Nation, or the Mexican Mafia. Although these gangs may have helped you survive on the outside, they will only hinder your new life as a member of Jesus' disciples.

There's an old gang saying, "Blood in, blood out." Typically, it means if you want to get into a specific affiliation, you have to kill someone from a rival gang to do so, and the only way to get out is in a body bag. The one exception to this rule I've observed in my 26 years of prison ministry is if a gang member has a radical conversion to Christ. Brazil's gang violence reached an all-time high in 2017 with 64,000 gang murders. The only legitimate way out besides death was conversion to Christianity. One gang leader told the Washington Post, "We aren't going to go against the will of God. God comes first above everything." An interesting side note on this policy is that some Brazilian pastors will report to gang leaders if the convert doesn't begin to live a Christian life.[iii]

Breaking old patterns means finding new people to model your life after. As Paul observed in 1 Corinthians 15:33: "Do not be deceived: 'Bad company ruins good morals.'" If you struggle with alcohol, you can't hang with your old bar buddies. If you have a gambling addiction, a friendly game of poker with the guys is probably not a good idea. Doing so will trigger old patterns. Our flesh (sinful nature) is very powerful and has a long memory.

One councilor described life as a long hallway with many doors. Each door represents an area of sin that is a struggle for us. Some of them are tightly closed. For me, the heroin door is shut because I have never tried heroin and by God's grace, never will. But in my hallway, the vodka door is wide open because I experienced pleasure, relief from inner voices, and the ability to interact from drinking it socially. Upon my release, I needed to steer far clear of the party crowd. I needed new friends who found pleasure, support, and connection through healthy, godly avenues.

Some of you might disagree with me regarding your old group of friends, thinking, *I can go and witness to them! I can get them saved, and we can still be bros.* Forget about it! Pray for them, and God will send someone to your old gang to witness to them besides you.

I use a physical demonstration with my congregation about keeping bad company. One person stands on a chair, and the other one stands flat on the floor. First, I tell the one standing on the chair to try to pull the guy on the floor up to their level. If they're particularly strong, they may be able to lift the person a few inches, but they give up after about ten seconds. Then I tell the one on the floor to pull the one on the chair down to their level. It usually takes only a couple of seconds to do so (and about half the time there are injuries involved). I have never seen a case where ex-cons go back to their old stomping grounds and succeed in converting their former gang associates to Christ. They always end up reverting to previous patterns.

> It's easier for someone to pull you down than for you to lift them up.

A New Commandment

In John 13:34-35, Jesus told his disciples, "A new commandment I give to you, that you love one another: just as I have loved you, you also are to love one another. By this, all people will know that you are my disciples if you have love for one another." Loving people was not a new biblical idea, but what made Jesus' command different was that he told his followers to love as he had loved them. What will it look like for you to seek friends on the outside? What will it look like to love them like Jesus?

Laying Down Your Life for Them

There are many types of people that come to mind when we think about someone laying down their life. Having just watched *Saving Private Ryan* not too long ago, I think about the men who lost their lives trying to take the beach at Normandy France on D-Day during WWII. Some might recall those men and women who gave their lives on 9-11, trying to save the people trapped in the Twin Towers. Dramatically, their lives ended in the line of what we call "duty." But is Jesus calling us to this kind of sacrifice? Are we to seek out ways we can heroically jump in front of a bus to save someone's life?

This kind of sacrifice is honorable, and we need to recognize those who do this, but I don't think this is what the Lord had in mind. He was talking about sacrificial living, where we set aside our desires at times, which is humbling, and attend to others. I want you to note that Jesus' new command doesn't limit us to attending to the needs of others, but goes so far to say interests also. One of the best ways to show love to your new friends is to get interested in what interests them.

My new friend Brian who visited me in prison was a collegiate diver. One of the activities we would do when I got out was going to the pool to hang out, and even though I had no interest in learning how to dive, Brian tried to teach me. It was pretty comical, and most days, I would gingerly limp back to the locker room with the skin on my chest glowing bright red from all the belly flops I had done. Conversely, I had taken an interest in golf after my release, and Brian would go with me to the driving range and even golfed a few rounds with me. Either one of us could have said, "I don't like doing the activity you've chosen. You go ahead, and I will watch." Instead, we took an interest in the passions of the other person. Sacrificially preferring the activities others enjoy truly demonstrates the love of Christ.

One way Brian exemplified this was in our nightly conversations back in the Lundin's basement. He would sit and listen to me go on and on about my desire for a wife, seeking his opinion about the different young women we both knew. "What do you think of this one? Would she make a good wife?" Though Brian did not have marrying interests at the time, he patiently cared about helping me make great choices in this critical area of my life. And when I began to date Mary, who would become my wife, my primary attention naturally shifted to her versus my best buddy Brian. This transition was not easy for him, yet he was in full support of our future together. It was because of Brian's sacrificial friendship that he was my best man at my wedding. In those times, he loved me like Jesus, laying down his life for me, and I am forever grateful to him for that.

Bearing with Friends' Weaknesses

People can be very annoying. Most often, the problem is they are not perfect. In psychology, there has been a very consistent observation when it comes to how humans deal with other people's shortcomings and weaknesses. We are hard on others but easy on ourselves. The very flaw we overlook in our character we criticize in the people we love.

Paul encouraged the church in Ephesus concerning this propensity toward being harsh and judgmental. He said, "I therefore, a prisoner for the Lord, urge you to walk in a manner worthy of the calling to which you have been called, with all humility and gentleness, with patience, bearing with one another in love, eager to maintain the unity of the Spirit in the bond of peace." I believe the only way we can bear with one another's weaknesses is to recognize we all need grace from others.

I'll never forget a conference I attended that spoke about the Heavenly Father's heart toward His children. During the meeting, the main speaker wanted all the spiritual leaders to come forward and sit on chairs near the front of the auditorium. He then called for anyone who felt they had been wounded by their earthly fathers to come forward. In one of the most awkward, yet profound, ministry moments I have ever experienced, he had us sit on the laps of those spiritual leaders. The leaders began to pray for the wounding that our biological fathers had inflicted upon us and were instructed to listen to the Holy Spirit's voice regarding that hurt. Before his legs went completely numb from my 220-pound girth, one of my pastors told me the Lord wanted me to know that my biological dad didn't leave me because he was mad at me or because he was a bum. It was because of his pain and complicated relationship with his own father.

At that moment, I realized I had been angry with my dad for a long time, not comprehending he needed grace from me. He needed me to bear with his shortcomings in love. Remember that it was while we were still sinners that Christ died for us. It was while we were still a mess with tons of shortcomings that Jesus took the massive step of reconciliation toward us.

As you begin to make new friends on the outside, you may not experience a colossal hurt that you need to forgive in others. You may have dozens of small offenses that slowly build up toward them; for example, your friends don't pay their fair share of the bill when you go out to eat, or they decide as a group to go to a movie you have no desire to see.

All these small offenses can lead us away from loving one another and can jeopardize our relationships. Don't sweat the small stuff. People are complicated, and you can never be sure why they act the way they do. You may think they have intentionally done something to slight you, but in reality, they probably have some deeper issue they are working through. Be quick to forgive. Remember the words Jesus taught us to pray: "Forgive us our trespasses, as we forgive those who trespass against us" (Matthew 6:12).

Avoid Theological Battles

On the inside, I found many of my new friendships developed around studying the Bible and finding common ground with other Christian inmates. Often, we would sit for hours discussing a particular theological point. At times, the intensity of those arguments was somewhat surprising. Upon hearing all the commotion emanating from our cells, the guards probably wondered if they needed to call the goon squad to break us up and throw us in solitary to cool down. However, no matter how volatile the disagreements, we never let it get in the way of our friendship. Those quarrels seemed to strengthen our bond. It was kind of like basic training in which we would practice fighting each other to prepare ourselves for a future war. As new Christians, we were testing our weapons.

One of my best friends in prison was John. He was serving time for murder after he killed a man in a drug deal gone bad. I met John when I first arrived at the prison in St. Cloud, Minnesota, and my first impression was he was one of the cockiest people I had ever encountered. He wasn't a Christian, and it showed in his arrogant attitude. He had been in for eight years at that point, and he seemed to look down on anyone new to life behind bars. I had been in the honor cell block for a few months when the guy in the cell next to me transferred to another prison. I contemplated who my new neighbor would be and thought to myself, *Let it be anyone but John.*

The next day, John moved in, barely giving me a condescending glace on the way past my cell. I inwardly groaned thinking it was going to be a long two years! What made it even worse was he was close friends with all the Christian guys that had taken an interest in my conversion. About two months after John moved in, I became a Christian and the Lord started to soften my heart concerning my new neighbor. One night, I felt God prompting me to pray for John. I went over to the wall between our cells and laid

> God prompted me to pray for John instead of hate him.

my hands on it, lifting one of the weakest, faithless prayers I had ever prayed: *"Jesus, if it's even possible, I pray you would somehow save John."*

To my shock, John became a Christian within a couple of weeks of that prayer. He started joining in on our Bible studies, and the intensity level went through the roof. John was a battle-hardened con who had scrapped his way up the ranks of the prison population. As an unbeliever, he had typically used aggression and intimidation to make his point. Some days I would walk out of a brother's cell after a particularly passionate doctrinal scuffle feeling like I was bleeding. It was invigorating! My Bible knowledge developed by leaps and bounds because I didn't want to look weak. I would study for hours in my cell so I could beat John in the discussion the next day. That first paperback New International Version prison Bible was tattered and marked up from cover to cover.

Like soldiers who have shared the same foxhole during a terrible war, John and I became very close friends. He was released from prison about five years after me, and my wife and I invited him to come live with us. At his wedding, I was his best man, and he even went on to name one of his eight sons after me. Many inmates will have similar stories to tell about their friendships on the inside. The prison environment seems to produce these kinds of relationships. However, on the outside, battling over theology is not received as well. It's scary to most Christians, especially in a relativistic world where people get uncomfortable if you tell them they are wrong about what they believe.

When the Kinship group first formed, I learned pretty quickly that my new friends' eyes would begin to glaze over, and they would start fidgeting in their seats if I launched into a passionate doctrinal discussion. When you start to make new friends on the outside, don't expect the same kind of intensity you may have experienced with your brothers on the inside. In some ways, it's like the soldier that comes back from war and tries to adapt to life as a civilian. The tactics and habits that helped them survive on the front lines do not translate into post-war life. Their intensity might scare friends and loved ones, so they need to learn how to face day-to-day challenges in a calm manner.

Finding New Friends

Chances are you will probably not meet someone like Lizabeth at a prison concert who connects you with new friends on the outside like Brian and Mark. In the area you are paroled, you might not know any Christians; thus, you will need to seek them out. As you attend your new church, small groups are a place to meet new people and develop some meaningful relationships. If you are under the age of 25, a young adult group is a great option. My oldest son, Peter, just moved back in with us a few months ago after being away for two years. He found that most of his high school friends had moved away to college, so he didn't have anyone he could call and hang with. Our small church doesn't have a young adult ministry, so I encouraged him to begin to attend a group at a larger church in Monterey. The very first week he was there, he connected with some guys that have adopted him into their inner circle.

If you are older, you can seek out friendship in what some churches call Life Groups. These are groups that meet weekly to have fellowship, study the Bible, and worship together. We live out the Christian life in communities, and in many ways, these small groups are like a family. The New Living Translation of Psalm 68:6 says, "God places the lonely in families; he sets the prisoners free and gives them joy." You will find freedom and joy as you interact with your newfound family in the Lord. He will help you as you seek him because he wants you to succeed on the outside, and he knows you cannot do that in isolation.

Tips for Family and Friends

Tip #1 – Encourage Your Newly-Released Loved One to Seek Out New Friends

If a prisoner paroles to their hometown, they may gravitate toward reconnecting with their friends from the old gang. DO NOT encourage this! Don't call up their old buddies and throw a getting-out-of-jail party for them at your house. Instead, begin to do some research for your loved one about different small group options at churches nearby. You may even want to attend a few of these groups to see if they are a good fit. Remember, most guys on the inside don't have access to the internet, which is the primary way to search for groups in the modern world. Have a shortlist available of times and locations these groups meet upon their release.

Tip #2 – Don't Let Them Isolate

Many inmates turn to isolation on the inside as a survival tactic. Doing so might seem like a safe option for them on the outside, but it will only lead to depression and cause them to long for their previous life back on the inside. Don't let them sit around your house and watch TV or play video games. If they are going to live with you for a short period when they get out, make this one of the ground rules. Initially, you will probably have to drive them to a group until they get their license and save up enough for a car. Public transportation is also a great option. Usually, once they get involved in a group, they shouldn't have a problem getting a ride from one of the attendees.

Questions for Discussion

1. What are some of the things you are going to miss about being on the inside?

2. Are there any church groups with a prison ministry at your location that you would be interested in checking out when you are released? What about them appeals to you?

3. Where will you live when you first get out? How long do you plan on being there?

4. Will your most significant challenge be isolation or reconnecting with the old gang when you get out? What are your strategies for overcoming those temptations?

5. Do you have someone on the outside who can do some research for you about small group options in the city in which you will be paroled?

6. What are the ways friendships on the outside will be different than the ones on the inside?

7. Imagine walking into a small group for the first time. How does that make you feel?

Beware of Romantic Relationships

"He who finds a wife finds a good thing
and obtains favor from the Lord."
Proverbs 18:24

"Women weaken legs."
Mick, Rocky

From the time I was in junior high until about two years into my prison sentence, I was never without a girlfriend for more than a week. Amid the struggle to connect with boys my age, I discovered that girls were attracted to me. I don't know if it was because I was so pathetic and they felt sorry for me, or if it was my incredibly good looks (ha!), but I never had trouble finding a girlfriend. One relationship would end and within a few days, I would be on a quest for the next heart I could bond with for consolation. I was not emotionally healthy and gravitated toward unhealthy representatives of the opposite sex. My success in winning their affection was one area that made me feel wanted, and it boosted my bruised self-esteem.

The last relationship that fit this harmful pattern was with a woman named Michelle. We had been dating for about nine months when I was arrested. In a healthy, normal relationship, my incarceration would have ended that romance immediately, but because of our dysfunction, Michelle stayed with me for two years into my prison time. She was my lifeline to the outside world. She came to visit me at least once a week, and we wrote to each other almost every day. We would even have long conversations on the phone whenever I had the chance to call her.

Michelle came to see me for the last time in 1993 on Christmas Eve. I knew something was wrong when she walked into the visiting room because her mascara was smudged. She sat down across from me on the cheaply upholstered government-issued chairs and took my hands in hers. She confessed she had cheated on me and was seeing another guy. I had been bracing myself for this for months because I had noticed some changes in her behavior. Her letters were less frequent and felt distant. Plus, she was visiting less often. I knew it was time to let her go so she could have a healthy life with someone else on the outside. I had a year and a half left to serve, and it was unfair to expect her to wait any longer than she already had. I told her I understood and hugged her, but as she turned and walked out of St. Cloud Correctional Facility, she was sobbing.

After she disappeared, I walked over to a side room to be searched for contraband and then retreated to my cell and flopped on my bunk. I could hear Christmas music echoing through the cell block from another inmate's TV. I knew my siblings on the outside were probably getting ready to open their presents and pass around the eggnog. It was the lowest point of my life. Even though that moment hurt like crazy, I am so grateful Michelle dared to break off our relationship. It was in that moment with nothing else to cling to that I began to turn to Christ. He allowed me to feel the pain of that loss so that I might realize how dependent I had become on women to make me feel significant. God wanted me to understand it was only in him that I would find myself.

Prison Girlfriends

I would love to tell you that as soon as I became a Christian, all my unhealthy patterns regarding relationships disappeared. That was not the case. If the opportunity had presented itself, I would have immediately sought out another romantic connection. Thankfully, my remaining time in prison allowed me the chance to mature in Christ a bit. That preparation time helped me make some tough choices when I got out.

I spoke earlier about Lizabeth, a young lady who came into Lino Lakes Prison a few months before my sentence ended to perform in a concert. The beneficial result of that encounter was my connection with the Kinship Group. The detrimental part was that Brian and Mark were not the only friends she told about me. When she returned home after the concert, she immediately called her friend, Kimberly. About a week later, the two of them came to visit me. My desire to get married was compelling, and Kimberly seemed like just the kind of Christian woman I was seeking. After the visit was over, she asked if she could write to me, so I gave her the address of the prison along with my inmate ID number.

She began to correspond with letters every day, and a romance quickly blossomed. Looking back now, I should have been able to read the signs that this was just another unhealthy relationship disguised in Christian clothing. Even though I had grown spiritually over the previous eighteen months, no one had taught me about what it meant to be a godly boyfriend or husband yet. I thought because we were Christians, God would work everything out for the best. I was dead wrong.

Kimberly and I went out on a date within a couple of days after my release from prison. The location was the Lake Harriet bandshell in Minneapolis. It was May of 1994, and love was in the air, or something like it. I realized within the first hour of our date that Kimberly had the gas pedal to the floor in her heart. The Spirit of the Lord was telling me to run, and thankfully he gave me the strength to do so before we went way too far.

The next day I called Pete Lundin. That was when we had our famous Perkins conversation about discipleship. I spilled everything to him about Kimberly, and he rightly perceived I needed significant help in the area of romantic relationships. He saw I lacked an understanding of how marriage worked. My natural father should have modeled this, but in his absence, my knowledge was severely deficient.

I have spoken with dozens of inmates about the issue of prison girlfriends. About half had girlfriends they were dating before their arrest and, like Michelle, they'd stuck with them during their incarceration. The other half somehow obtained girlfriends while in prison, like I had with Kimberly. There are numerous reasons I have tried to talk inmates into ending the relationship, but I will focus on three of them.

Maintaining a Relationship in Prison is Unfair to the Woman

Looking back now, I cringe to think of what I put Michelle through. St. Cloud Prison was 70 miles from her apartment, and she dutifully made that journey almost every week. What a waste of time for her! She should have focused on her own life. Instead of spending all of that energy on me, she could have been seeking out her future husband. I had nothing to give her. I wasn't making any money to speak of; in fact, she frequently sent me money.

Think of all the time those women on the outside spend worrying about their prison beau. They lie in bed at night, wishing they could be with them or spend countless hours writing letters of encouragement to them. They walk with them through the trials and troubles of prison life, concerned about the safety and well-being of their incarcerated boyfriends. Prisons go on lockdown quite often, and when that happens, the relationship goes on hold until the warden decides the security issues have been addressed. This seclusion can go on for weeks, sometimes months.

A woman needs romance. She wants to go out on dates to restaurants and movie theatres. She wants Christmas gifts from her man. She wants to feel like she is unique, and it's nearly impossible for a guy on the inside to provide this experience for her. Under certain circumstances, prisons will allow the inmates to have a conjugal visit with a girlfriend, but think of how degrading that must be. "Hey honey, come down to the jail so we can have sex in a shack next to the guard tower. Oh, by the way, there will be a corrections officer right outside the door just in case anything goes wrong."

> Women need romance and prisoners can't provide that.

If You Were Her Father, You Would Not Be Happy About the Situation

I was in a men's group meeting a few months after I got out of prison when a man told me he felt the Lord had impressed upon him a message about how women should be treated. He said, "Scott, God wants us always to remember that these potential mates we meet are his daughters first and foremost." That has always stuck with me. It is even more prevalent now that I have a 17-year-old daughter of my own with guys who are interested in dating her. I have certain expectations when it comes to how I want Cassie treated in a relationship. God's expectations are even higher than mine.

I know I would be appalled if my daughter came home one day and said, "Hey, Dad, I have a guy that wants to date me. He's great, the only problem is he's in prison." Heck no! I would not be blessing that relationship. Many convicts forget that the bond they established with a woman extends to her family. I haven't met anyone who was happy about their daughter being the girlfriend of a prisoner. I would venture to say, I probably never will. Speaking to the guy still in prison, would you want your daughter dating you? If you are honest about it, the answer is a resounding no.

Outside Relationships Distract you from Your Main Focus

One of the biggest challenges those on the inside face is doing time. Each morning, they wake up knowing exactly how many months they have left until they regain their freedom. They want each day to pass as quickly as possible, so they try to fill their time with diversions. These distractions include things like working out, reading, watching TV, and playing cards. A relationship with a woman on the outside can also be a distraction. It gives the inmate hope and connects them to the real world.

Although this attachment may help the time go by more quickly, it distracts from their issues. An inmate's main goal should be self-rehabilitation. The way they accomplish this is by attending Bible studies, participating in twelve-step programs, spending time with their brothers in Christ, and reading. Convicts carry lots of baggage. They have emotional and spiritual problems that contributed to their crimes. They need to spend most of their free time working on those issues.

Self-reflection is not fun, but it is crucial to success on the outside. If the prisoner thinks he or she can wait until their release to deal with these problems, they will be in for a rude awakening. The more they can process through their junk on the inside, the better off they will be once they hit the streets. There will be plenty of other things to focus on once they are out.

Taking Time to Discover Who You Are

When I moved in with the Lundins, the primary area of concern for Pete was my dysfunction in the realm of romantic relationships. We spent hours talking about God's design for marriage. One evening, a few months after this mentoring had begun, we were sitting in the living room and I said something I would later regret. "Hey Pete, I don't trust my judgment when it comes to dating. I promise not to ask a girl out unless you give me your blessing." He smiled, then chuckled. "All right, you've got a deal." Little did I know how long it would be until I received that blessing.

For the next two and a half years, I spent a significant amount of time with the Kinship Group, and many beautiful single Christian women attended as well. I thought any one of them would make a great wife. After an event, I would go back home to try to convince Pete I had found "the one." I would go on and on about how great each woman was, her exceptional Christian character, and her love for God. However, Pete would always say the same thing: "Let's take a season of prayer and fasting and see what the Lord has to say about it." We went through this on many occasions, and each time we both concluded the timing wasn't right and I wasn't ready.

I was quickly down about 20 pounds from all the prayer and fasting, and I was beginning to think I was never going to find a woman that would receive the blessing from Pete and the Lord. Back when I first moved in with the Lundins, I was sitting in their living room with a bunch of my guy friends from the Kinship Group, discussing life. This group would later become known as the Brotherhood (See Chapter 7). Just then, there was a knock at the door. A young lady named Mary had come to visit Sandy. Pete answered the door, and in walked one of the most beautiful women I had ever seen. We all stood as Pete introduced her. She apologized for interrupting our meeting and made her way to the kitchen, shutting the door behind her.

> In walked the most beautiful woman I had ever seen.

After the group concluded and all the guys had left, I gave Pete a sly smile and said, "That Mary is amazing." His face quickly clouded over, and he said in no uncertain terms, "Don't even think about it." That seemed to put the kibosh to any ideas I had about approaching her. She and I didn't hang out in the same circles, but now and then I would see her when she came over to visit with Sandy or at special church events the Lundins invited me to. Whenever I saw her, I would hear Pete's voice in the back of my mind. Eventually, she began to date another guy, so I laid my interest in her to rest, figuring she was spoken for.

Fast-forward two years. I was sitting at the kitchen table one day having lunch with Sandy. A funny little smile came to her lips and she said, "You know, Mary and John broke up." Suddenly, the clouds parted and a ray of sun poked through! Maybe this was why I had been waiting all this time. Perhaps she was the one, and the feelings I had that first time I saw her were not just false hope.

I was a little nervous about approaching Pete, as I remembered his stern warning, but I figured I had the backing of his wife this time. That evening when he came home from work, I spoke to him about what Sandy and I had discussed earlier. I said, "I know you said, 'Don't even think about it.' Do you still feel the same way?" He responded, "Scott, you were a different person two years ago. Let's take a season of prayer and fasting about how to move forward with Mary." And move forward we did because he and Sandy met with her about a week later, and without bringing up my name, they asked her opinion concerning dating. She said she needed a little time to recover from her last relationship and finish her degree, but by November she would be ready to consider dating again. It was February, and when the Lundins told me what she had said, I was a bit deflated. I had waited what seemed like an eternity to begin a relationship, and now I had to wait ten more months to even talk to Mary!

I decided that I needed to do something to distract me from thinking about her, so I started training for the Chicago marathon, which was in October. This goal helped me release all my pent-up energy with running. Even with that, the time seemed to drag on. Eventually, November 1st arrived and over my lunch hour at work, I called her. There was an instant connection, and we decided to go out for lunch the next day. From that moment on, we were inseparable. We spent every spare minute we had together. We took long walks, went to the movies, ate in restaurants, and drank way too much coffee in local shops. Four months later, I proposed to Mary, and we set a date for June.

The question for you to consider is why the Lord had me wait three years to find the one to marry. I think part of it was because I didn't know who I was or what my life's direction would be. I needed to discover the path that God had ahead for me before I invited someone else along for the journey. You might think you have it all together on the inside; you might even be a leader among your peers. Nevertheless, life on the outside has many challenges that are very different from those behind bars. Your path toward a romantic relationship will look very different than mine, but there are a few core issues that will be the same. The following principles are non-negotiable in creating a healthy relationship.

No Ring, No Ring-a-ding-ding

I first heard these words from Tom Brock, former lead pastor at Hope Lutheran in Minneapolis, as he was addressing a group of confirmation students, encouraging them to consider God's plan for sex. Now, the ring he was talking about was not an engagement ring; it was a wedding band. Most guys in prison were sexually active before they were incarcerated, but then they found themselves in jail and had to stop cold turkey. As soon as they are released, the temptation to jump right back into bed with a woman is compelling, even for Christians. Joel Young, a chaplain from Soledad prison in California, told me this is one of the main challenges he faces with the guys he mentors. He tries to convince them that sex outside of the marriage covenant is a big mistake. The Bible strictly forbids fornication (sex with someone who is not your wife) and adultery (sex with another guy's wife). I found two things that helped me immensely to resist sexual temptation.

Fight Pornography

After I was saved, I eliminated all pornography from my life. Before I was a Christian in prison, I had a pile of it in my cell. The corrections facility sold porn magazines in the inmate store. As soon as I placed my trust in Christ, I threw it all in the garbage. You should have seen those other inmates pathetically scrambling to dig through the trash upon seeing me do this.

Looking at pornography stirs the sexual drive. At first, a man may be content to just look, but eventually he begins to seek out ways to fulfill the fantasies that porn feeds. Unfortunately, pornography is rampant in our internet-driven society. As I sit at my computer writing this, I know if I wanted to view porn, I wouldn't need to disguise myself hoping no one sees me as I go to some sleazy adult bookstore to buy it like in the days before the internet. Now it's just two clicks away. To protect me from the ease of access, I have accountability software installed on my computer that sends a report to a chosen personal friend. If he sees anything suspicious, he emails me to check in to see if I am struggling. I also have two pastor friends that I can call if I am in the heat of a battle with lust. They do not judge me, but they receive my confession and declare to me the promises of God: "If we confess our sins, he will forgive us of our sins and purify us from all unrighteousness" (1 John 1:9).

Don't Spend Time Alone in Romantic Settings

When Mary and I began to date, we spent as much time in group settings as possible. She lived with her brother and his family, so I was at their house a lot. We tried to limit alone time in romantic situations. We hung out in the living room rather than her bedroom. We decided not to stay out too late, knowing the later it was, the weaker our resolve became. We did not entirely live up to our ideals, but through wisdom and God's grace, we were able to make it to our wedding night without falling into sexual sin with one another. This practice set a foundation for the rest of our marriage in the area of intimacy. It helped build trust because Mary knew I was able to resist having sex even when the desire to do so seemed overwhelming.

I recognize that for some of you, these last few paragraphs will stir up feelings of guilt and shame because you have not successfully navigated the rocky waters of sexual purity. Don't despair! The purpose of guilt is to draw us closer to God, not make us hide away in shame. Confess your sins to him and start over. If you are in a relationship and have had sex, go to the one you love and commit to purity moving forward.

Tips for Family and Friends

Tip #1 – Even if You Didn't Walk in Sexual Purity When You Were Young, Encourage it for Your Loved One

The sexual revolution of the 60s and 70s was a major disaster. America sowed the wind of free love and is reaping the whirlwind of broken homes. Divorce is rampant, and sexual promiscuity is a badge of honor among many teens today. Like me, you may have made many bad decisions in this area as a young adult. These failed decisions might make you feel like you are unqualified to tell your son or daughter to restrain their sexual passions and wait for marriage. I, on the other hand, would advise just the opposite. The fact you experienced the negative results of unrestrained desire gives you exceptional credibility. If I believed making mistakes disqualified me from encouraging others not to make the same mistakes, I wouldn't be writing this book or ministering to those in prison. I've found that my criminal past has afforded me even more credibility with the incarcerated. They realize I know what I'm talking about when it comes to the negative consequences associated with crime.

Talk to your kids about sex. Don't leave them wondering how you feel about it, and whatever you do, don't think pop culture and the public-school system will teach them what they need to know. These two entities are firmly in the grasp of the enemy who wants to destroy us through misinformation, causing us to question God's wisdom in this vital area.

Tip #2 – Don't Present Sex as Something Dirty

The Devil can never create anything new, but can only twist what God has made into something it was never intended it to be. Sex is a beautiful gift given to humanity for our enjoyment. We are to enjoy it within the boundaries of the marriage covenant. Telling your children or those you are mentoring that sex is dirty is like telling them they shouldn't do drugs because they aren't fun. The first time they try drugs, they will know you are lying and won't trust your advice from that point forward. I tell my kids that sin is fun and exciting. But remember, Satan disguises himself as an angel of light (2 Corinthians 11:14).

I am also candid about the negative effects of sex outside of marriage. I tell my children stories about how sin in my life led to severe natural consequences. My openness doesn't always deter them from dabbling in sin, but when they do stumble, they know they can come to me for counsel because I have been honest with them.

Questions for Discussion

1. What are some of the unhealthy patterns you observed in your family growing up?

2. Are you currently in a relationship with someone on the outside? How did it start?

3. How are you doing in the area of sexual purity concerning pornography? Do you have an accountability partner you can talk to about your struggles?

4. Do you plan on having sex as soon as you are released? What are your thoughts about what the Bible has to say about fornication and adultery?

5. Do you think Pete Lundin made Scott wait too long before he gave his blessing on a romantic relationship?

6. What are some of the negative consequences you have seen in your life from past sexual relationships?

7. Where did you learn most of what you know about sex?

Part II
Spiritual Growth

Take it Slow

"But when you are invited, take the lowest place,
so that when your host comes, he will say to you, 'Friend,
move up to a better place.' Then you will be honored in the
presence of all the other guests."
Luke 14:10

"Wisely and slow, they stumble that run fast."
Friar Laurence, Romeo and Juliet

The first month I was out of prison, I attended a church gathering in a community park building in downtown Minneapolis. We were handing out hotdogs to homeless people, and afterward, we had a time of worship, prayer, and testimonies. I had a burning desire inside of me to get up and tell everyone my life story. I wanted people to know God had touched me and I was radically changed. The pastor leading the meeting could see my eager desire to do this (I was practically vibrating in my seat), so he asked if I had something to share. I jumped out of my chair, nearly bowling him over in my excitement to get to the front, and shared a condensed version of my prison experience and conversion.

The desire to give my testimony was, I'm sure, mostly Holy Spirit-led. Nevertheless, I also became aware of another desire that coexisted alongside that pure motive—my longing to be recognized. I had a deep need for validation as a significant part of the Body of Christ. I had leadership potential I was hoping people would see. I wanted to jump in and get to work because then I would feel important. If I could quickly get working, I could make up for all that lost time in prison, and in the process, hopefully, earn some brownie points with my Heavenly Father. Thankfully, my mentor, Pete Lundin, was at that meeting and he was able to reign me in gracefully.

Dealing with Rejection

Over the last 26 years, I have been ministering in many jails and prisons. I see the same patterns in those men that I had. They want to hit the ground running when they get back on the streets. They want recognition as leaders. They want people to trust them. They hope for the same kind of leadership position they enjoyed in the prison setting among their peers. However, they become frustrated when ministry leaders don't recognize their potential and welcome them with open arms into some critical role within the organization.

Rob Maho, a good friend of mine that I served time with, was rejected by two prison ministries that were initially excited about his interest in their work, but when they found out he was a felon they wanted him to wait for two additional years before joining them. This denial was after he had already been out and off of parole for four and a half years. So, Rob waited. Because of his patience, he was eventually invited to join a prison ministry team that conducts retreats in jails and prisons called Residents Encounter Christ (REC). So, instead of mentoring in a one-on-one capacity like he would have been in the first ministry opportunity, Rob now speaks into the lives of hundreds of men.

Rejection is common. Many ministries have been burned by parolees who have zeal for the Lord but also carry baggage from time in prison. They might not be reliable because they don't have sound biblical doctrine, and are very needy. Rob didn't let these rejections deter him. He kept seeking the Lord for the right fit for him. During that first six years, he participated in street evangelism, did outreach with Native American groups (Rob is Native), taught Sunday School, and used his carpentry skills to work on houses with a handy-man ministry in his church.

It might feel like your prison record will block you from walking through all the doors you desire, but we must remember the promise of Revelation 3:8, where Jesus tells the church in Laodicea, "I know your works. Behold, I have set before you an open door, which no one is able to shut." Particular doors may close for a certain period, but later those doors will burst wide open. Joseph was sold into slavery by his brothers right after he told them about a dream he had where they would bow down to him. As a slave, he was unjustly accused of attempting to rape his master's wife and was thrown into prison for ten years. I'm sure he probably felt like God had forgotten him, yet he didn't give up. Genesis 39:21 shows us that the Lord had not abandoned him: "But the Lord was with Joseph and showed him steadfast love and gave him favor in the sight of the keeper of the prison."

God humbled Joseph in prison. When he was young, the dream he had received from the Lord made him feel significant; instead of keeping it to himself, he ran to his family and bragged about how God was going to have them bow down to him. Now that many difficult years had passed, he was ready to fulfill the vision with the proper attitude. Joseph could be trusted to carry out God's plan to save many people through his servant-leadership.

Building Trust

Many places in Scripture tell us to trust in the Lord, but nowhere does it ask us to place our trust in man. Actually, it says just the opposite. During the time of Jesus' ministry, John 2:24 shows us his attitude towards those who flocked around him: "But Jesus on his part did not entrust himself to them, because he knew all people." Does this mean we should never trust anyone? Not necessarily. It just means we can only rely on people to a degree, never entirely. The adage is "Only trust a man as far as you can throw him."

We build trust over time based on the observation of correct decisions and faithful service. When your family and friends see you living for the Lord on the outside, they will begin to depend on you more and more. Trust is never something we should expect or demand; rather, it is something earned. Also, remember we can lose trust in an instant. One moment of weakness or one relapse can put us almost back to square one. Think what would have happened if Joseph had jumped on the opportunity to punish his brothers for selling him into slavery when they came groveling to him in Egypt, begging for food. They would have never trusted him again and probably would have rather died of starvation than accept his help. Slowly build up trust, and people will begin to give you more responsibilities.

Spend Significant Time with Your Family

During your first few years on the outside, your most significant ministry will be to your family. Recall how much you longed to be with them when you were on the inside. I remember some of the most challenging times for me in prison were during the holidays. I could imagine my family sitting around the Thanksgiving table, laughing and eating turkey, mashed potatoes, and cranberry sauce. One particularly difficult time was when my great-grandfather died and I was heartbroken I couldn't be there to support my family at the funeral.

Attend every family function that you possibly can, even if it means traveling a great distance. Doing so is especially crucial if they are non-believers. The tendency for many Christian ex-offenders is to gravitate towards the new set of church-friends they have made. The main reason for this is they share common ground and feel built up in their faith when they are around them. Time spent with non-Christian family members can be difficult because they know all about your past. They know who you were before your conversion, and being reminded of this can be humbling. So, the more time you spend with them demonstrating the new life in Christ you have found, the more authentic your faith will become. Notice how Joseph embraced his family when they came to him, even though it might have been tempting to disassociate with his modest past as a simple farmer.

Everything is Beautiful in its Time

In Ecclesiastes chapter 3, Solomon talks about everything being made beautiful in its time. As you start slowly by spending significant time with your family, take time to enjoy those lovely seasons as they unfold before you. Now, Solomon is not talking about the seasons of the year like winter and spring. He is talking about the seasons of life, or the aging process. He says there is a time to be born and a time to die. In the time that spans from birth to death, there are numerous seasons of life.

In my family, our children are in a season of departure. As their father, there is a mix of emotions, particularly pride in their accomplishments, but also sadness as I recognize the distance that will be between us. Once they transition out of the house, I will not be able to peek in on them sleeping at night like I have for the last 21 years. If God has blessed you with children, pour your energy into them by spending as much time with them as possible. Their childhood flies by in the blink of an eye.

Another thing Solomon says that relates to the aging process is that there is a time to be silent and a time to speak. As a minister, I have spoken many words in the 600+ sermons I've preached, but that season of continual speaking didn't come until I had been out of prison for 15 years. One of the things I find interesting about Jesus' ministry is that people rejected him during certain seasons of His life, but then accepted him at others. One particular group was His family. Mark 3:20-21 describes one such incident by stating, "Then he [Jesus] went home, and the crowd gathered again so that they could not even eat. And when his family heard it, they went out to seize him, for they were saying, 'He is out of his mind.'" In fact, in Nazareth, Jesus didn't speak much because they had very little faith. Jesus quotes the prophet Isaiah by saying, "Truly I tell you... no prophet is accepted in his hometown."

Solomon goes on to talk about beauty in changing relationships. One of the most astonishing realities of heaven is the relationships we have with those who have placed their trust in Jesus will go on forever into eternity. No more fathers abandoning their families or being sent off to prison. No more spouses running off with a newfound lover. No more goodbyes around gravesides.

While we grind out our day-to-day existence on earth, we find we begin to take people for granted by losing sight of their eternal worth, and we are annoyed by their habits and mannerisms. I have noticed this with my own family. There have been times when I was away at a conference or on a mission trip and when I returned all I wanted to do was spend time with my family. I wanted to sit and talk for hours about whatever was going on in their lives. In the routine of everyday life, I had forgotten how precious they are to me.

Finally, Solomon encourages us to see the beauty in chance events. Later in Ecclesiastes 9, he makes a curious observation. "I again saw under the sun that the race is not to the swift and the battle is not to the warriors, and neither is bread to the wise nor wealth to the discerning nor favor to men of ability; for time and chance overtake them all." The word translated as "chance" means to happen upon or to encounter as on a journey. In life's journey, you are going to happen upon many different encounters with good things and bad things. There are so many areas that fall into this category, but I will only name a few, so you get the idea.

- Your parents happened to meet each other, and you came into existence.

- You happened to be born in a particular era of time and a specific location.

- You happened to sustain a life-altering injury or succumbed to a particular disease.

- There just happened to be a certain job available at the same time you were looking.

- You happened to have your money in an investment account right before the market tanked, or went through the roof.

- You happened to meet and fall in love with your spouse.

The point is that so much of life is out of our control. The beauty about happening upon events in your life under the sun is that from God's perspective, these are not chance events. We know this from verses like Proverbs 16:33: "The lot is cast into the lap, but its every decision is from the LORD."

It's hard to think of a more chance event than a roll of the dice, but God determines every outcome. This truth should give us great comfort in what may seem like the most random events in our lives. So many things are going to be revealed to us in heaven about this life that we live here under the sun, things that might not make any sense at the time and might even cause us sorrow and confusion. But Solomon indicates that God makes everything beautiful in its time, including the seemingly wasted days you spent in prison. As I look back now on the four years I spent in the Minnesota Corrections Department, I can honestly say that season was beautiful in its time.

> **God determines the outcome of even the most random events.**

Tips for Friends and Family

Tip #1 – Give Them a Chance to Build Trust

Some of the guys I was close with in prison had done terrible things to their families and friends amid their criminality. Drug addiction caused them to steal from loved ones to support their habit, and fits of rage ended in verbal and even physical assaults. There was absolutely no trust between them and, if truth be told, they were glad to see their son, daughter, or friend head off to jail so the cycle of destruction could be halted. This mistrust is only natural because no one likes to be abused, and everyone needs to set boundaries around their lives to protect themselves.

One thing I have learned in my years of prison ministry is that everyone deserves a second chance. You need to decide what that second chance looks like to you. When they get out, your first step of trust-building might be meeting them in a public place, such as a restaurant or coffee shop. This small step may be as far as your boundaries will allow you to go. Pray, and then trust your instincts, but my greatest encouragement is not to write them off completely. Even the most hardened felon can change when the Holy Spirit begins to transform their heart and mind.

With that being said, I should also add a warning. Extending trust to the newly released prisoner may not include things like inviting him or her into your home, loaning them money, or letting them use your vehicle. It may take a long time observing their progress to get to the point in which you feel comfortable with these things. Much of this depends upon how long they have been Christians and how strong your relationship was with them before they got out. Were you consistently visiting them while they were still incarcerated? If so, you may have a pretty good sense of where the relationship is currently.

Tip #2 – When Your Loved One Gets Out, Try Not to Push Too Hard

Many family members may be tempted to see the time their loved one spent in prison as "wasted years." The family will be anxious to see the ex-offender start to make up for lost time by jumping right into the rat race on the outside. However, family members might not be aware of how slow things are inside prison. There are long periods locked in cells with nothing to do but read, hours spent in the yard just walking in a big never-ending circle and the reality that every morning you wake up knowing exactly how many days you have until your release.

Most ex-offenders struggle with the chaos of life. There is a great scene in the movie *Shawshank Redemption* in which Brooks Hatlen has been in the Shawshank prison for almost five decades as the inmate librarian. Upon finding out he is going to be paroled to the streets, he has a mental breakdown by grabbing a shank and attempting to cut the throat of one of his prison buddies. With the blade pressed to the man's throat, many others gathered around to talk Brooks out of it. Brooks attempts to commit a crime so he might remain in prison. After much coaxing, he finally caves to the reasoning of his friends and puts down the shank.

Afterward, the others gather in the prison yard to talk about what happened. Morgan Freeman's character, Red, gives some meaningful insight to the prison mindset. "He's just institutionalized. The man's been in for 50 years. In here, he's an important man, an educated man. Outside he's nothing. Just a useless con with arthritis in both hands." The year is 1955 when Brooks gets out, and on the first day, he almost gets run over by a car because there were only horses and buggies on the road when he entered prison.

Some inmates who are released today will have never owned a cell phone or been on the internet in their entire lives. They need time to adjust to the pace, so give them time and don't push too hard. With a sound support system, they will find their rhythm and begin to cope with the changes.

Tip # 3 – Celebrate Small Victories Together

Although you may want to see the parolee jump right in and begin a career, get married, or start a family, it's the small accomplishments they will be most proud of in those first few months. One such accomplishment for me was renewing my driver's license. I had been in long enough that it had lapsed, and I needed to retake both the written and driving test. I hadn't driven a car in four years, and I was sweating bullets as I tried to parallel park while the test administrator scribbled notes on his clipboard. Passing was a huge victory for me, and my grandparents celebrated it with great enthusiasm.

For your loved one, it might be that first job or figuring out how to buy gas with a credit card. In some ways, you have to treat the releasee like a teenager relearning life skills we adults take for granted. Instead of becoming frustrated with their lack of knowledge about the basics, go out for a celebratory latte when they clear each new hurdle. By the way, you might have to explain to them what a latte is because prison coffee is a pretty big step down from Peets.

Questions for Discussion

1. What are some of the things you are hoping to accomplish in your first three months after you get out? How about in your first year or five years? Are these reasonable goals?

2. Will the fact that you just got out of prison be something you will share publicly, or will it be something you desire to keep private? Why?

3. As you think about building trust, what are some practical things your friends and family will be looking for that will help that process? How do you feel about this necessity for building trust?

4. Do you want to get involved with prison ministry when you get out? If so, why?

5. Rob Maho was rejected many times as he attempted prison ministry and wasn't able to go back in for six years. What are some other areas of ministry you could see yourself getting involved in besides prison ministry?

6. What are some necessary life skills on the outside that you foresee giving you cause for concern?

7. What are things you look forward to doing with your friends and family upon your release?

Join a Good Church

"Not neglecting to meet together,
as is the habit of some, but encouraging one another,
and all the more as you see the Day drawing near."
Hebrews 10:25

"The Bible knows nothing of solitary religion."
John Wesley

Since we moved so much when I was a kid, I attended many different types of churches. Somehow my Mom knew she would be able to find the support she needed in these congregations. This, coupled with the fact that in prison I attended many services hosted by numerous church groups, caused me to gain a comprehensive view of the current religious landscape. It made me realize that one particular denomination didn't have a corner on the market regarding Christianity.

It also helped me realize there are problems in every church and I would not find a perfect one when I got out of prison. Local congregations cannot be all things to all people because the Lord gives each church a particular personality. Some churches are like hospitals, only focusing on healing the spiritually wounded. Others predominantly focus on equipping families by offering a variety of classes on the challenges that come with marriage and parenting. Still, others concentrate primarily on outreach and are very concerned with the homeless, even offering twelve-step programs for those struggling with addictions. When you hit the streets, one of your priorities will be to find a church that fits your current needs.

Reasons You Need to Attend Church

The Psalms mention assembling with the congregation 20 different times. Psalm 111:1 says, "Praise the LORD! I will give thanks to the LORD with my whole heart, in the company of the upright, in the congregation." It continues by giving three main reasons for us to ensure we are seated in a pew on Sunday morning.

We Study the Works of the Lord

If there was anyone in the Bible who had seen the mighty works of the Lord, it was David. He saw God skip over all of his older brothers and choose him as the successor to the throne in Israel. The Lord used him to defeat the mighty Goliath. He also outwitted Saul numerous times in his attempts to kill him. Yet David did not just sit back at home thinking about all the things the Lord had done for him. Instead, he joined the congregation to study the mighty works God did in the past and continued to do in the lives of his people. Not only did he examine God's actions, but he also studied God's work, that great work of salvation.

The Bible calls us God's sheep and, like sheep, we easily forget essential things. We need reminding over and over again.

When I was a kid in Wisconsin, I contracted myself to dairy farms to earn extra money by helping with the milking. Periodically, the farmer I worked for would buy a cow that was mature and had belonged to another farm. The biggest problem I had in my job was getting the new cow into their milking stall. At the previous barn, they may have been in a particular spot, but in the new barn we wanted them in a different location. No matter what we did, that dumb cow would continually go to that same old spot for months, even though there was another cow already standing there! It was only by repetition that she would finally go to the correct stanchion.

People are the same way. Even though we've been saved, our flesh wants to go back to that old criminal life. We need to be led over and over again to the right spot. The Bible is filled with stories of people just like us, and when we attend church, we are encouraged as the pastor preaches about the heroes of the faith.

God Provides for Those Who Fear Him

Psalm 111:5 goes on to state, "He provides food for those who fear him." When you get out, God's primary way of providing for you will be through the congregation. Did you know the majority of nursing homes and hospitals were ministries of particular churches before the 18th century? Acts 4:34-35 shows how the New Testament church provided for its own. "There was not a needy person among them, for as many as were owners of lands or houses sold them and brought the proceeds of what was sold and laid it at the apostles' feet, and it was distributed to each as any had need." We cannot fix

> God's primary way of providing for you will be through his people.

unemployment in America, but we can sell that field (whatever form that takes) and lay it at the apostles' feet (the offering plate) so that we might care for the Body.

We See God's Power and Faithfulness

The final reason given for assembling is the most important. God indeed works in our daily lives to show his power and faithfulness, but throughout history, we see him work primarily through congregations. Even missionaries who have gone out to do amazing things in the power of the Lord were sent from churches.

A while back, I picked up a book at the thrift store for 49 cents entitled *Rich Dad, Poor Dad*. One reason this author states we should work to become rich is we will have the power to do things and buy stuff with our wealth.[iv] I suppose that is correct in an earthly sense. But the kind of power I long to see cannot be bought with money. It is the power to change lives. It is the power to fix marriages. It is the power to overcome death. Money alone cannot accomplish these things, as is seen in the disastrous lives of the rich and famous.

Biblical preaching that stays true to sound doctrine has amazing power. As the words leave the preacher's lips, they are transformed mid-flight by the power of the Holy Spirit into arrows of hope, piercing the heart of the listener. God gifts the preacher with the power to proclaim those kinds of messages, then his Spirit impacts people's lives and evokes change. How are we going to see that kind of display of power while we sit home or attend a sporting event on Sunday morning?

Don't isolate yourself from God's people. But you might say, "The people at church are a bunch of selfish, egotistical hypocrites." As my old pastor, Tom Brock, used to say, "Always room for one more!"

The Importance of Doctrine

The Church in America is going through major doctrinal shifts. Some mainline denominations have departed dramatically from orthodox teaching to the point they deny the virgin birth, the resurrection, the authority of the Bible, and the existence of hell. As you search for a local congregation to call your home, it will be vital for you to research their doctrinal stance. Orthodoxy should be the standard of biblical truth by which any Christian church measures its correctness. By straying too far to one direction or another, entire denominations have crossed over into heresy.

Not all churches are going to agree on gray areas like the exact timing of eschatology (the study of the end times), but they should, at a minimum, adhere to the Nicene Creed (See Appendix A). There are five fundamental areas you will want to investigate to determine if a church is heretical or not.

Does the Church Believe God is the Creator?

The first section of the Nicene Creed states, "We believe in one God, the Father Almighty, Maker of heaven and earth, and of all things visible and invisible." Because of the prominent teaching on evolution, many have begun to call into question the creation account in Genesis. One of the biggest arguments from evolutionists against Biblical creationism is their perception of a universe that is billions of years old instead of thousands of years like the Scriptures indicate. But let me pose this question: Upon seeing Adam in the Garden of Eden minutes after his creation, what would you have guessed his age to be? Probably closer to 15,768,000 minutes old (the number of minutes it takes to get to 30 years old) rather than one minute old. We can apply this age perception phenomenon to the earth. Just because it appears older than 7,000 years doesn't mean it is. God created it with a word out of nothing into a fully formed ecosystem, according to Scripture.

Does the Church Believe in the Deity of Christ?

The main controversy dealt with at the Council of Nicaea had to do with the deity of Christ. Is Jesus truly God or just a created being sent to save us? Again, we turn to Scripture, not our human understanding, to find the answer. Consider the following biblical proofs:

- The Bible calls him God – John 1:1, "In the beginning was the Word, and the Word was with God, and the Word was God."

- His role in creation – John 1:3, "All things were made through him, and without him was not anything made that was made."

- Accusations of blasphemy against him – Mark 2:7, "Why does this man speak like that? He is blaspheming! Who can forgive sins but God alone?"

- He receives worship – Revelation 5:8, "And when he had taken the scroll, the four living creatures and the twenty-four elders fell down before the Lamb, each holding a harp, and golden bowls full of incense, which are the prayers of the saints."

- He claims attributes of God – Revelation 1:8, "'I am the Alpha and the Omega,' says the Lord God, 'who is and who was and who is to come, the Almighty.'"

GET OUT FOR GOOD

Does the Church Believe in the Humanity of Christ?

The next portion of the Nicene Creed presents the necessity of believing that Jesus, although fully God, condescended to become an actual man. He came down from heaven, was conceived by the Holy Spirit, and was born of the Virgin Mary. These beliefs might seem pretty basic, but one of the first significant controversies in the early church had to do with this very doctrine.

The heresy that crept into the church in its infancy was called Gnosticism. The central dogma of the Gnostics was that material things were evil, and spiritual things were good. To achieve salvation, one only needed the correct spiritual knowledge to transcend the evil physical world. How this affected Christianity was that many began to believe Jesus did not actually become flesh and blood, but only adopted the appearance of a man while remaining a pure spiritual being.[v]

What does the Bible say? 1 John 1:14 makes it clear that Jesus was an actual man with a beating heart and vulnerable body: "The Word became flesh and dwelt among us..."

Does the Church Believe in the Sacrifice of Christ?

Humanism is the belief that, with enough education, sacrifice, and teamwork, humanity can save itself from itself. This fallacy has wormed its way into the church in what is called the social gospel, which is no Gospel at all.

Here's a bold statement for you—we can't save the planet! The reason it's doomed is not because of climate change caused by carbon emission, the oceans filling up with garbage, or overpopulation. God wants us to be good stewards of the world he has given us, but ultimately, HE is going to destroy it with fire someday. 2 Peter 3:10 reads, "But the day of the Lord will come like a thief. The heavens will disappear with a roar; the elements will be destroyed by fire, and the earth and everything done in it will be laid bare."

The devil knows this, as he can read Scripture. He quoted it to Jesus to try to tempt him. So, he knows if he can distract the church away from our real need, which is the salvation of our souls based on the sacrifice of Christ, and turn it to our temporary earthly problems, he has won a great victory. As the Nicene Creed affirms, we must believe he suffered under Pontius Pilate, was crucified and was and buried. Paul stated he desired to preach nothing but Christ crucified. I think he would be sad and angry if he visited many churches today where the devil has effectively removed the Gospel message.

Does the Church Believe in the Resurrection of the Dead?

During the time of Jesus, there was a great battle among the religious leaders. The Pharisees believed the soul was resurrected after death, but the Sadducees believed this life was all there was and nothing beyond. The heretical churches would have you believe the same thing. *"Let us eat and drink for tomorrow we die."* But what is the greatest hope for the Christian? Titus 2:13 states, "While we wait for the blessed hope—the appearing of the glory of our great God and Savior, Jesus Christ." If you are waiting for God to give you a perfectly happy life here and now, you are going to be very disappointed because life is going to deal you your fair share of pain and heartache.

> This life is going to deal you your fair share of pain and heartache.

The resurrection of our frail bodies is a fantastic promise. The fact that we get to live forever on a new, sinless earth should be of great encouragement. You can reassure yourself, I can get through today because I know this life is not all there is. Paul longed to die and be with the Lord. His "best life now" was defined by suffering and sacrifice, not upgrading to a faster, more luxurious private jet.

The Importance of Tithes and Offerings

During my incarceration, I worked in a barbershop making 80 cents an hour. After I became a Christian, I heard a preacher on the radio talking about tithes and offerings. He said giving monetarily to a local church was crucial to the spiritual life because, as Jesus said in Matthew 6:21, "For where your treasure is, there your heart will be also." I began sending money out to a congregation that was holding chapel services in our prison. I've always wondered what that church bookkeeper thought of my $12.80 check each month. From that meager beginning, I have continued the practice of giving tithes and offerings since the day the Lord saved me over 28 years ago.

When you join a local congregation, begin giving right away. A news report came to my attention some time ago regarding a severe threat to a church in Arkansas.

> "Little Rock detectives arrest and charge three suspects with the robbery of a church congregation Sunday. Reverend Elmo Johnson from Third Baptist Church describes the fear of being robbed at gunpoint but says he finds comfort now that it's all over. Little Rock Police Chief Stuart Thomas says this is a significant event. 'Being robbed in a church is extraordinary. You don't typically see that type of boldness and cruelty.'"[vi]

Indeed, this is a terrible crime, but Malachi 3:8-11 describes another robbery taking place among the people of God.

> "Will man rob God? Yet you are robbing me. But you say, 'How have we robbed you?' In your tithes and contributions. You are cursed with a curse, for you are robbing me, the whole nation of you. Bring the full tithe into the storehouse, that there may be food in my house. And thereby put me to the test, says the LORD of hosts, if I will not open the windows of heaven for you and pour down for you a blessing until there is no more need. I will rebuke the devourer for you, so that it will not destroy the fruits of your soil, and your vine in the field shall not fail to bear, says the LORD of hosts."

This verse is from the Old Testament, and so we must ask the question, does the New Testament instruct Christians to give 10% (tithe means tenth) of their income? Let's examine what Jesus said about the issue in Matthew 23:23. "Woe to you, scribes and Pharisees, hypocrites! For you tithe mint and dill and cumin, and have neglected the weightier matters of the law: justice and mercy and faithfulness. These you ought to have done, without neglecting the others."

His point was they tithed even down to the spices they received, but they were ignoring justice and mercy. Now, Jesus was not saying forget about the tithe. He stated, "...these you ought to have done," meaning practicing justice and mercy, but then he continued with "...without neglecting the others," indicating tithing. Notice when Jesus deals with those who would try to pin down the list of what they were to do to earn God's favor, he always went beyond the commandment by getting to the heart of the issue.

Regarding adultery, he told them if they looked upon a woman with lust, they had committed adultery already with her in their heart. It's the same with the issue of tithing. Jesus essentially said, "Let's bring this giving up to a new level." When the rich young ruler went to him to try to find out how to be saved, Jesus saw how connected his wallet was to his heart and told him to sell EVERYTHING and give it to the poor, not just 10%. One of the greatest indicators mentioned in regards to Zacchaeus' salvation was when he said he was going to give half of his possessions to the poor. And why did he offer to do this? Was it because Jesus pulled out some Old Testament laws and gave him a bunch of rules? No! It was because Jesus had saved him! He was overwhelmingly thankful.

One man who was proud of the fact he was a tither asked a pastor friend of mine how much he should give. Pastor Tom Parrish responded, "Jesus isn't the least bit interested in the percentage of your income that you give back to his mission. Jesus is only interested in how thankful you are for all he has given to you." Pr. Tom later found out that right before his death, this man was giving around 50% of his income to the Lord. I guess he realized he was pretty thankful for all that God had done in his life.

Those young men who robbed that church in Little Rock, Arkansas had their day in court before an earthly judge and most likely spent some time in jail because of their crime. However, when we rob God, there is a different consequence. According to Malachi 3:9, the result is a curse upon your finances. But God wants to bless your finances, and he even says to put him to the test (one of the only places in Scripture) to see if he will not pour out blessings from heaven.

Would you rather rob God and live with 100% or your income under God's curse, or live with a bit less (maybe 87% or even 50%) and be blessed by God? I have seen this principle work amazingly in my life, but I need the Holy Spirit to help me in this area because I am naturally tightfisted.

Tips for Family and Friends

Tip #1 – Don't Argue Doctrine

Prison exposes inmates to many different doctrinal beliefs. In my experience, the conversations about this subject get pretty intense on the inside. Unless you see your loved one slipping into heresy, it's best to let them sort out their beliefs with their newfound church friends. In that way, you can remain a supporter rather than becoming an adversary.

Tip #2 – Consider Your Giving Practices

We lead best by example. If you want to see the ex-offender prosper in the area of finances, become a case study as to how God blesses those who are obedient with their resources. This transparency can be a little tricky because we should be giving in secret, according to Matthew 6:4. Without judging, try talking with them about your giving and how the Lord has affected you through this practice.

Questions for Discussion

1. What are some of the experiences you have had in church settings that have shaped your view on congregational-life?

2. What are some of the current needs in your life you are hoping to have met by the church you chose?

3. Are there other reasons not mentioned by Scott you believe show the importance of church attendance? Which one resonated with you the most on the list he shared?

4. Briefly share with the group a testimony of how God has impacted you through the Body of Christ.

5. What are some of the most controversial doctrinal issues you have come up against in prison?

6. About which area of the Nicene Creed do you have the most questions? (See Appendix A)

7. Do you agree with Scott's views on tithes and offerings? Why or why not?

Acquire Accountability

"Therefore, confess your sins to one another and pray for one another, that you may be healed. The prayer of a righteous person has great power as it is working."
James 5:16

"An accountability partner is able to perceive what you can't see when blind spots and weaknesses block your vision. Such a person serves as a tool in God's hand to promote spiritual growth, and he or she watches out for your best interest."
Charles Stanley

In the last decade, there has been some groundbreaking research in the area of sheep behavior. Dr. Andrew King of the Royal Veterinary College of London explained the findings. In the experiments, they strapped GPS collars on the sheep and then monitored their reaction to a perceived threat, in this case, a farm dog. They found that sheep are always trying to find the safest place, which is at the center of the flock. They know those on the outside of the circle get picked off by predators, which is why wolves attempt to scatter them.[vii]

But sometimes the wolf doesn't even need to scatter the flock because one sheep will wander away and become easy pickings. There are many reasons that sheep do this; perhaps they're so focused on the juicy grass in front of them they fail to realize the group is heading in the opposite direction. Once they're lost, their weak vision causes them to wander around aimlessly. Soon the sheep may find themselves feeding on poisonous plants and unhealthy water.

James 5:19-20 says, "My brothers, if anyone among you wanders from the truth and someone brings him back, let him know that whoever brings back a sinner from his wandering will save his soul from death and will cover a multitude of sins."

Anyone Can Wander Away

First, notice James is speaking to believers about those who might wander away. He says, "If anyone among you wanders," which shows Christians can wander. As the great hymn says, "Prone to wander, Lord, I feel it. Prone to leave the God I love." The reason we are prone to wander is because of three things: the world, the flesh, and the devil. This ungodly trifecta is trying to pull us away from God. The world does this by tempting us to sin and chase after those things that are not of God, like riches, fame, and glory. Our flesh is the sin nature we're born with and rebels against God's law. The devil is our great adversary and is continually trying to kill us and destroy our lives. He will tempt us like he did Eve in the Garden of Eden by lying about God's Word.

There has been much debate down through the centuries about whether or not someone can lose their salvation. I believe there is biblical support for each side of this issue, but regarding accountability I want to draw your attention to the passages that warn Christians to take heed lest they fall away. Scripture compares the relationship between the Christian and Jesus to that of a bride with her husband. That bride needs to continually keep the promises she made in the marriage vows. If she decides to cheat on her man, it will have a devastating effect on the relationship. In the same way, God wants us to be faithful to him because he knows we are going to be secure and filled with joy when we do.

Consider what happened to Israel when His holy people continued to be unfaithful to him with foreign gods. Jeremiah 3:8 says, "I gave faithless Israel her certificate of divorce and sent her away because of all her adulteries." These were the people of the covenant. From God's side, he had kept all of his promises to care for them and never leave them, but they kept cheating on him with foreign gods. The wandering Christian is tempted to leave the protective care of the Chief Shepherd. In so doing, they expose themselves to needless pain and hardship, just like a cheating spouse leaves the protective care of the marriage covenant.

This decision doesn't typically happen overnight. It occurs over months and even years. Satan is patient, and he will continue to work on an individual by trying to separate him/her from the flock. Once he does, they become easy prey. Listen to the Lord's warning about the impact wandering from the congregation can have as he speaks to the church in Laodicea. "So, because you are lukewarm and neither hot nor cold, I will spit you out of my mouth." If we want to be used as Jesus' mouthpiece, we need to stay connected to the true vine.

We also see the need to continue the race with perseverance. Paul states in Galatians 5:7, "You were running well. Who hindered you from obeying the truth." Someone lied to the new Christians by telling them in order to be saved they needed to be circumcised. Paul encourages them to keep running the race that has been set before them. The devil intends to lie to you and hinder your race, sometimes, even using the words of supposed Christians.

The Need for Accountability

Like sheep, people do much better in social situations where they interact with others. This tendency is why we need accountability. When I got out of prison, I began to meet regularly with Pete Lundin, my spiritual mentor. Those meetings were so productive that I began to invite other young guys to join us every week. This group became known as the Brotherhood. We would check in about the challenges we faced and the sins we battled. After someone shared, the rest of us would give advice from Scripture about how to overcome whatever they were fighting. We would stand with them in prayer and call them during the week if they needed encouragement. We helped prevent them from wandering from the flock.

Pastor Tom Parrish speaks about the need for accountability in his Foundations course. He says accountability requires leaders and followers to be aggressive in soliciting input and correction and be diligent in making necessary changes in their lives. We accomplish this by living in the light, while being open with our failings, doubts, and sins before God and our accountability agent, which, in my case, was the Brotherhood. The pastor goes on to say that resistance to accountability comes from five primary sources.

GET OUT FOR GOOD

A Spirit of Rebellion

1 Samuel 15:23 says, "For rebellion is as the sin of divination, and presumption is as iniquity and idolatry." That's a strong statement! Divination is defined as the practice of seeking knowledge of the future or the unknown by supernatural means. Scripture strictly forbids this method of determining your decisions for the future. Instead of seeking accountability from the body of Christ, many consult occult sources like tarot cards, psychics, Ouija boards, or horoscopes.

Behind each of these techniques, a demonic idol is lurking, trying to steal God's glory and lead you away from the flock. They may have the ability to provide you with specific information about your life, not out of love for you, but rather because they hate you. There is only one Good Shepherd, the Lord Jesus, who laid down his life for the sheep.

Ignorance

Hosea 4:6 says, "My people are destroyed for lack of knowledge" (the Hebrew meaning "cut off"). Notice it doesn't say, "Unbelievers are destroyed for lack of knowledge." As Christians, you can be destroyed because you don't seek godly counsel. When a sheep wanders from the flock, it strays from the protection the group provides. Corporately, the sheep are much less susceptible to attack, especially when guard dogs are watching over the flock.

> **As Christians, you can be destroyed because you don't seek godly counsel.**

As a shepherd, David killed a lion and a bear to keep them from raiding the sheep for a meal (1 Samuel 17:36). Mentors are like the guard dogs of the kingdom, and Jesus protects you by providing counsel that annihilates the marauding demons sent by Satan to steal, kill, and destroy (John 10:10). Remember, the devil prowls around like a roaring lion seeking whom he may devour (1 Peter 5:8).

Fear and Mistrust

In prison, I needed to be very careful about who I trusted. Associating with the wrong men could have led to severe problems, like getting stabbed. This fear is why some inmates do their time in isolation. They are fearful of being targeted if people discovered their crimes. Additionally, they fear if certain men find out what gang they were associated with, they might get taken out by a rival.

I have noticed in my life since becoming a pastor that I fear what people might think if they found out about my struggles against sin. The reason for this is that ministry is a unique occupation. At most other places of employment, the boss doesn't care what you do during your off time as long as you show up on time and do the required work. As a pastor, my whole life is on display; if I stumble into sin, no one is going to be laughing around the copy machine on Monday morning. I could lose everything I worked for in seminary, and I could do serious damage to my congregation. The enemy wants me to isolate to the point where I don't have anyone I feel I can turn to for fear of losing my position.

This kind of inaccessibility is deadly. It has led to many terrible train wrecks within the Christian Church. To counter this tendency, I have four pastors with whom I converse regularly about the challenges of ministry. I know I can tell them anything without fear of retaliation. I trust them, and they trust me because we are in the same position. I have confessed my sins to them (yes, even your pastor sins), and they have shared with me the promise of 1 John 1:9, "If we confess our sins, he is faithful and just. He will forgive us our sins and purify us from all unrighteousness."

Pride

Tom Parrish elaborates on pride in relation to accountability:

> "There are two types of pride. The first which is condemned as sin is a pride that seeks to advance or elevate ourselves over others, or to protect ourselves from change. It is this pride that prevents us from having a 'teachable' spirit. It hardens our hearts against advice and correction and ultimately against God.
>
> The second is the pride that rejoices in what others accomplish or the changes that God works in us. This kind of pride encourages us to open ourselves to others and to accept changes in our own lives. We are children of God, whom he loves, teaches, and entrusts with service and the Good News. We can and should take pride in this and his similar work in the lives of others."

Reactions to Past Abuses

One of the most significant problems with the Church is it is made up of people. While I was in the Brotherhood, I had some disagreements with other men in the group. One guy even quit coming because he didn't like the advice he received. Interacting with humans is messy because they are not perfect. They make mistakes.

Sometimes these mistakes go beyond the innocent kind. Some people are so broken that they shouldn't be in leadership, but somehow, they are able to hide their open wounds from others and suddenly have significant influence over God's flock. One such person was Jim Jones. As a staunch Communist and Marxist, he pondered how he could demonstrate his political agenda without being singled out by the U.S. government during the McCarthy trials. Then it dawned on him to infiltrate the church. He began a small church called the People's Temple in the 1950s, which grew over the next two and a half decades. He finally relocated what had, by that time, become a cult to Jonestown, Guyana, where he orchestrated a mass-suicide. Nine hundred eighteen people died, including three hundred four children.[viii]

There are many false prophets in the Church. Jesus warned about them in Matthew 7:15: "Beware of false prophets, who come to you in sheep's clothing but inwardly are ravenous wolves." Be careful when you choose your accountability partners. Ensure they are the kind of people who have your best interests in mind and can keep confidential matters to themselves. One good indicator is whether they are open about sharing their sins and shortcomings, or if they present themselves as the perfect example you should follow.

Bringing Them Back Saves Their Soul

In James 5:20, Paul states those who wander have wandered from the truth. There are two aspects to the kind of truth from which they may have strayed. First, they may have wandered from doctrinal truth, and they believe a lie. This attitude is hazardous to the soul of the believer.

Let's consider an actual scenario that was taking place in Paul's day that he addressed in another letter to Timothy. He tells the young pastor that some have been spreading false doctrine. In 2 Timothy 2:18, we see the result: "They [the false teachers] have left the path of truth, claiming that the resurrection of the dead has already occurred; in this way, they have turned some people away from the faith." They claimed Jesus had already returned, and everyone that was going to be resurrected had already been. This belief shipwrecked the faith of many people. Do you see how dangerous false doctrine can be and how wandering away from real understanding can place your soul in peril? Accountability, attending Bible studies, and listening to good preaching helps protect you.

How would this look if you were a sheep? Perhaps it would be compared to a sheep seeing a seemingly greener pasture over the fence. That grass looks so much tastier than the same old stuff they've have been munching on their entire life. A false shepherd may lure the sheep into crossing over the boundary line with the sole intent to slaughter them once they get into his territory. Satan wants to destroy your faith.

The second way a Christian can wander from the truth is through behavioral error. Galatians 2:14 says, "But when I [Paul] saw that their conduct was not in step with the truth of the gospel, I said to Cephas [Peter] before them all, 'If you, though a Jew, live like a Gentile and not like a Jew, how can you force the Gentiles to live like Jews?'" Peter's actions show he was not in step with the truth, and Paul confronted him. We need to do this with our fellow Christian brothers and sisters. When we see they are not behaving like sheep but rather are acting like a rebellious goat, their Christian witness is in danger. They need us to warn them and help them back into the fold.

Bringing Them Back Covers Over a Multitude of Sins

Some church bodies have a hard time calling Christians sinners. They say we are saints only, and to call ourselves sinners ignores the fact that we have been bought with a price and are seated with Christ in the heavenly realms. But I want you to note that even Paul calls himself the chief of sinners in 1 Tim 1:15. Even in the previous James passage, it is a brother in the Lord that we are trying to bring back from his wandering ways. We know this by the phrase in verse 19, where James says, "If anyone **among you** wanders…" (emphasis mine).

Although the New Testament focuses predominantly on the fact we are saints, there is still an indication that we are sinners at the same time, to one degree or another. The reason this impacts those who have wandered, and we all wander in our Christian walk, is because we are never beyond the Shepherd's reach if we are willing to look up when we hear the voice of Jesus through a fellow believer calling us back to the flock.

Confession and Absolution

In the church that I pastor, we include regular times of confession and absolution right in the service. Consider the following:

> Together, let us pray
>
> **Congregation** - Dear heavenly Father, I confess that I have sinned against You with my actions, my words, and even my thoughts. I ask for Your forgiveness and seek Your great mercy. I come before You trusting that Jesus' death on the cross was for my sins. Wash me, cleanse me, and forgive me that I may be pure and holy in Your sight. This I ask in the name of Jesus, my only Savior.
>
> **Leader** - It is in the strong and powerful name of Jesus that I proclaim to you who do truly believe His promises that you are fully forgiven

of all your sins. This I proclaim to you in the loving name of God, the Father, Son, and Holy Spirit.

Amen

During the Last Supper, Jesus did something very significant. He washed the feet of His disciples. When he came to Peter, an interesting conversation unfolded. "He came to Simon Peter, who said to him, 'Lord, do you wash my feet?' Jesus answered him, 'What I am doing, you do not understand now, but afterward, you will understand.' Peter said to him, 'You shall never wash my feet.' Jesus answered him, 'If I do not wash you, you have no share with me.' Simon Peter said to him, 'Lord, not my feet only but also my hands and my head!' Jesus said to him, 'The one who has bathed does not need to wash, except for his feet, but is completely clean.'"

As Christians, we stumble and get our "feet" dirty. When we confess our sins and seek absolution, all the sins we pick up in the midst of walking this road of life are washed away. Our confession can happen in a church setting, but more importantly, it can happen with individuals of our choosing. James 5:16 says, "Therefore, confess your sins to one another and pray for one another that you may be healed. The prayer of a righteous person has great power as it is working." Our sins are like a sickness threatening our spiritual health. Keeping them to ourselves only causes them to fester and become infected. The wounds need to be exposed and cleansed.

Just recently, I stumbled in an area I have struggled with my entire life. It was embarrassing because I feel that after all these years of serving the Lord, I should be beyond this particular sin. I decided to talk with the council president of our church. I was worried because I didn't want to disappoint him, yet relieved when he told me he had his own battles and was thankful I had gotten things out in the open. He committed to pray for me and told me to text him the word "oops" if I fell again in the future. I felt total love and understanding and was so thankful I had talked to him.

Those in Christian leadership can become so isolated that they feel like they need to present a perfect life to their congregations, but notice the Bible is filled with embarrassing stories of people's failures. This should encourage us to know we are not alone in this struggle with sin if we dare to bring it into the light.

> **Those in Christian leadership can become isolated.**

Tips for Family and Friends

It is difficult seeing your loved one wandering from the fold. The following list comes from the son of John Piper, the well-known pastor of Bethlehem Baptist in Minneapolis. Pastor John's son, Abraham, was a prodigal that had wandered from God. Upon his return to the fold Abraham gave the following advice about prodigals:

1. *Point to Christ* – The person's real problem is not drugs, homosexuality, or crime. It's that they don't see Jesus.
2. *Pray* – Only God can save your child by drawing them to Jesus.
3. *Acknowledge something is wrong* – Don't pretend everything is okay. Begin to treat them like an unbeliever that needs the Gospel message.
4. *Don't expect them to be Christlike* – Making them attend church or do Christian things will only make them into a hypocrite, not an authentic Christian.

5. *Welcome them home* – Don't shun them because they have chosen not to follow God. It is only through maintaining the relationship that you will have a chance to speak into their lives.
6. *Plead with them more than you rebuke them* – Be gentle in your disappointment. Stand firm but be kind about it.
7. *Connect them to other believers* – Chances are their eyes are just going to glaze over if you tell them for the hundredth time that they need to come back to God.
8. *Respect their friends* – If you don't accept the friends they have made, they will just go to other people that will.
9. *Email them* – If you find an encouraging article about what they are struggling with, send it off with a note saying you love them and are thinking of them.
10. *Take them to lunch* – Restaurants are neutral territory, and there is much less of a chance of having an argument that melts down into a screaming match.
11. *Take an interest in their pursuits* – Jesus spent time with tax collectors and sinners, and he wasn't even related to them.

Questions for Discussion

1. Why do you think the Bible compares Christians to sheep instead of a smarter, more noble animal?

2. Have you ever felt the desire to wander away from the Lord? What triggered that feeling for you?

3. Which of Pr. Tom's reasons for avoiding accountability resonated with you the most?

4. Do you have a group of friends that you can tell anything to and trust that they will not share it with those outside the group?

5. How does it make you feel when you hear that Scott struggles with a besetting sin?

6. Why is confession so hard to do?

7. Why is confession so critical to a healthy life in Christ?

Do Your Devotions

"But he would withdraw to desolate places and pray."
Luke 5:16

"A Christian without prayer is just as impossible
as a living person without a pulse."
Martin Luther

One of the main principles of army training is repetition. The drill sergeants would have us practice disassembling and reassembling our M16 rifles over and over again so we could practically do it blindfolded. We did PT (physical training) three times a day so our bodies could quickly respond during combat readiness exercises. If we had a spare minute between instruction sessions, our soldier's manuals and training guides would come out. These disciplines ensured that, in the heat of battle, we would instinctively know what to do.

Spiritual warfare is similar. Pastor David Johnson of Church of the Open Door in Maple Grove, Minnesota, puts it this way. "You cannot prepare for the evil day in the evil day." There are disciplines you will need to incorporate into your daily life to ensure your survival on the outside.

Bible Reading

King David was well aware of the training necessary to win battles, both physical and spiritual. Tradition says he used Psalm 119 to teach his sons the alphabet. Each new section begins with a new letter. Besides teaching his sons letters, King David also wanted to show them the rigors of the spiritual life. Psalm 119:9-16 is the section that begins with the letter "B". The Hebrew phrase is "Ba meh yezakkeh?" It translates into the question, "In what way can I stay clean?" This is a question you will be asking as you begin your new life in the real world.

When our four children were little, this was a question we asked ourselves all the time. How in the world are we going to keep them clean? Whenever we would get them all dressed up in a cute outfit and take them out to dinner or to a church function, before long it seemed like they would have a big smear of chocolate frosting on their clean white shirt. In the course of the evening, they would inevitably spill a bunch of Kool-Aid on their pants as well.

There were three main ways we would try to accomplish this monumental task of keeping them clean, and they resemble ways of staying spiritual clean as found in Psalm 119: "How can a young man keep his way pure? By guarding it according to your Word. With my whole heart, I seek you; let me not wander from your commandments! I have stored up your Word in my heart, that I might not sin against you."

GET OUT FOR GOOD

Guarding Them

Guarding the cleanliness of our children usually came in the form of a bib. The best bibs we found were the kind that were made of plastic and fit over practically their entire front. Some bibs had a pocket like a kangaroo that would catch any food that slid down onto their lap. Before the meal began, we would strap on this food shield to guard them from stains.

In Psalm 119:9, David tells his son he can keep his way clean by guarding it according to the Word. God's Word is meant to be a shield for you. It will teach you about the way of faith. Romans 10:17 tells us that faith comes by hearing and hearing by the Word of God. The more you understand the Scriptures, whether through studying or listening to others, the more you will be able to shield yourself from the filth of the devil.

Ephesians 6 is well known for its instruction on spiritual warfare. In verse 6, Paul instructs, "In all circumstances take up the shield of faith, with which you can extinguish all the flaming darts of the evil one;" The devil is continually launching flaming darts of doubt at believers. He knows if he can get us to question the truth of the Bible, it is only a matter of time before we begin to wander from the faith. Filling your mind with Scripture and meditating on God's precepts is a surefire defense against the relativistic thought so prevalent in the world today. Modern gurus will tell you there are no absolutes; what is right for one person may not be right for another. All paths eventually lead to God. In military jargon, this would be like saying, "It doesn't matter what side you're on, just as long as you fight."

WWII is an excellent example of how false this notion is. Even most modern Germans will tell you Hitler was a madman. Many of his goals were straight from the pit of hell, and those in the Nazi party who blindly followed him were brought to justice for war crimes during the Nuremberg trials. We rely on the truth of God's Word to guide us in how to live, not the propaganda of Hollywood.

One morning, when I arrived for work at my church, there was a car parked in the lot. I could tell someone was sleeping in it. I let them continue sleeping, but as I worked, I watched out the window to see if anyone emerged. Finally, a young couple got out and started rearranging their car. I walked over and introduced myself and asked if they got a good night's sleep. I offered them the use of our bathrooms and a fresh cup of coffee, and later I showed them the sanctuary where we talked for about half an hour. They were from Germany and were students who were taking a road trip around the United States.

I told them a little bit about the history of our church and then asked if they had any spiritual beliefs. Their answers were very typical of what I usually get. The guy, Thomas, said, "I believe in positivity and that everything happens for a reason. I don't believe there is just one god but that there must be something out there. I just hope for the best and treat others well." He went on to say he didn't have a single friend back in Germany who he would label 'religious.' However, his reasoning was flawed for several reasons.

> His reasoning was flawed for several reasons.

First, it was very vague. He had no real commitment to a particular belief system but rather held to a general belief in a generic higher power that is unknowable. Secondly, Thomas believed that just because he didn't go to church, he is not religious. The fact he had some kind of belief in God, no matter how vague, made him religious because the definition of religion is "the belief in and worship of a superhuman controlling power." If you believe in fate, you are religious. Finally, the reason he believed everything would work out well is based on karma. If I do good to others, good stuff will happen to me. Without knowing it, these young people were prisoners of war being held captive in Satan's camp.

Keeping Them Close

Another way our kids seemed to get themselves the dirtiest was by wandering off to play and ending up in a pile of mud, or worse. One of our children, who will remain nameless, went off once with his little friend, and they both took off their dirty diapers and began to smear them onto the white carpet in our bedroom. They were not very clean when we found them.

A few months later, I was walking through the Mall of America, and I saw the most fantastic invention. It was a kid harness. It resembled a dog leash for kids that secured them with shoulder straps like a backpack. At first, I thought, "That's just cruel." But immediately, I said to Mary, "We've got to get one of those!" We purchased one the next week, and sure enough, we were able to keep our wandering toddler much cleaner and out of trouble by keeping him close.

In Psalm 119:10, David cries out to God, "Let me not wander from Your commands!" This was his heart for his sons. He wanted them to stay close to God by following the commands outlined in the Bible. Reading the Bible is not enough though. You have to want to follow God with your whole heart. During your time in prison, you had quite a bit of time to dedicate to reading Scripture. When you get out, the demands of life will begin to put a squeeze on that time. You will need to make a plan that will allow you to set aside time each day to hear from God through his Word.

Filling Them with Good

I asked my youngest son, Seth, for permission to share this story. Ever since he was little, he had a problem with throwing up in the middle of the night. Because he is such a sound sleeper, he rarely made it to the bathroom. Talk about a mess! My wife and I spent countless nights cleaning up the carpet, bedsheets, and bathroom floor. But one day I thought to myself that maybe it had something to do with eating sweets after dinner. After discussing it with Mary, we started giving Seth his desserts at lunch instead of the evening, and sure enough, the problem stopped.

For you to stay clean spiritually, you need to be filled with good things instead of junk. Verse eleven of Psalm 119 says, "I have stored up your Word in my heart." Are you filling yourself up with junk that is causing you to vomit unclean things? If so, the old saying, "You are what you eat," indicates the reason.

King David's instruction to his young sons reminds me of a song I learned in Sunday school when I was a child.

> *Read your Bible, pray every day*
> *Pray every day, pray every day*
> *Read your Bible, pray every day*
> *And you'll grow, grow, grow*
> *Neglect your Bible, forget to pray*
> *Forget to pray, forget to pray*
> *Neglect your Bible, forget to pray*
> *And you'll shrink, shrink, shrink*

I've discovered I need to schedule my devotions first thing in the morning. If I put it off until later in the day, I get distracted or too tired to focus. You might not be a morning person and find the evening works best for you. The main point is to schedule the time. Don't just do devotions when you feel like it because you will find it challenging to be consistent.

Prayer

Bolette Hinderli was a simple country girl from Scandinavia. One morning she was praying near the ocean and she received a vision of a man in a prison cell. She sensed from the Lord that this man would follow in the footsteps of many other prisoners; he would get out and continue his life of crime, and eventually return to prison unless someone took possession of him in prayer. Bolette took this as a challenge from God and began to pray for him every day, even though she had never met him and didn't even know his name.

Years later, she was visiting Norway, where she heard a former prisoner was scheduled to speak at a church. When she arrived at the church, she took her place in a pew. She wondered if this was the man for which she had been praying. During the service, the pastor introduced Lars Skrefsrud, calling him forward to speak. When he walked past Bolette, she recognized him as the man in her vision. During his message, Lars spoke of his criminal life but then went on to relate how the Lord had called him out of his life of sin and equipped him to become an evangelist.

Lars Skrefsrud became an influential missionary in India, leading tens of thousands to Christ. Bolette Hinderli never saw Lars after that church meeting, but she continued to pray for him her entire life. At times, she would sense he was facing a difficult challenge as a missionary, and she would spend extra time interceding. These Christian warriors have both passed on to receive their heavenly reward, and I'm sure Lars was surprised when he met Bolette in glory and understood how crucial her prayer life was to his success.

Similarly, I had someone that took possession of me in prayer during my incarceration and continues to pray for me to this day. Her name is Sharon Wundrow and she is the mother of my high school sweetheart. Not only did she pray for me, but she also wrote me letters while I was still wandering from the Lord. Sharon and Bolette's example highlight the importance of prayer.

Paul instructs us in Ephesians 6:18 that we should be "praying at all times in the Spirit, with all prayer and supplication." Prayer is simply a conversation we have with God throughout the day. We can talk to him about anything that concerns us, and he has promised he will answer our prayers. Even though this dialogue can happen anytime and anywhere, it is also essential to set aside specific times for intentional prayer. Jesus modeled this during his ministry.

It's clear Jesus was continually conversing with his Father, as is seen in John 11:41-42: "And Jesus lifted up his eyes and said, 'Father, I thank you that you have heard me. I knew that you always hear me, but I said this on account of the people standing around, that they may believe that you sent me.'" The father-son conversation was on-going, but as a human being, Jesus was affected by the crowd's demands, so he often withdrew for an intimate time of prayer, as seen in Mark 1:35: "In the early morning, while it was still dark, Jesus got up, left the house, and went away to a secluded place, and was praying there." If the son of God needed time away from the busyness of life in prayer, how much more so do we?

GET OUT FOR GOOD

I am convinced the devil spends most of his time trying to convince people not to pray or when they do pray, it is ineffective. The reason for this is because he cannot stand against it. When we pray, we are recognizing our weakness and asking God to take charge.

For those who struggle to know what to pray, there are two methods I have used to assist me. The first uses the acronym TRIP.

- **T**hanksgiving - Give thanks to God for the day, for what he is doing in your life, or for an area where he has answered your prayers.
- **R**epentance - Ask the Lord to reveal areas you have fallen short in your Christian walk.
- **I**ntercession - Pray for others. This could be people you know or even those you don't, like government officials, our military, or the persecuted Church.
- **P**etition - Pray for yourself. You are asking God to provide for the things you need.

The second aid makes use of your hand as you pray for others. It's called the Five Finger Prayer.

- Thumb – I pray for those closest to me.
- Pointer Finger – I pray for those who guide us: teachers, doctors, clergy, counselors, social workers, and mentors.
- Middle Finger – (tallest one) – I pray for those who stand tall: government, civic, and business leaders, police, and firefighters.
- Ring Finger – (your weakest finger) – I pray for those who are weak: the poor, sick, infirm, infants, homeless, and the powerless.
- Pinkie – (the smallest, the least) I pray for my personal needs.

Walking through these prayer exercises might take you 10-15 minutes. Remember that even the most dedicated athletes had to start somewhere. Success on the outside is virtually impossible without prayer.

Fasting

In the world of dieting, many fads come and go. Currently, intermittent fasting is all the rage. Beyond physical benefits like losing weight, fasting is also commanded in Scripture as a part of our Christian life. It's probably not the most popular subject to bring before the people of God, as the reasons are apparent. Our flesh does not like to be deprived of comforts and screams bloody murder when that comfort is something we can control, like food intake. Jesus established the practice of fasting in Matthew 6:16. "And when you fast, do not look gloomy like the hypocrites, for they disfigure their faces that their fasting may be seen by others. Truly, I say to you, they have received their reward." I want you to notice that Jesus said *when* you fast, not *if* you fast. So why would Jesus want us to fast? How is it that fasting and not feasting on a triple cheeseburger seems to draw us closer to God? Here are a few reasons I see in the Bible.

> Our flesh screams bloody murder when we deprive it of comforts.

It is Humbling

James 4:10 says, "Humble yourself in the sight of the Lord, and he will exalt you." God is calling us to humble ourselves so he doesn't have to humiliate us. He desires to exalt us, but we are just too proud. Our flesh gets fat and satisfied and thinks that everything is lovely. But now try to go a day or two without food and see how wonderful that flesh feels. It will tell you quicker than you can say, "Jack Robinson," how you are impatient and crabby.

Our flesh is very powerful and does not like deprivation. But when you fast, you humble yourself before the Lord and also can discern more clearly the things he is trying to tell you. Remember that fasting doesn't always mean abstaining from food; you may choose to fast from media or something similar.

It Helps You Overcome Other Temptations

If you are struggling with sexual temptation, fasting from other things will help you because both the temptation to overeat and the temptation for unbridled lust come from the same place—the flesh. When we discipline ourselves, we gain power over earthly temptations. That little kid inside of us who wants to stuff his face full of Twinkies needs to be told "NO" now and then.

It Causes You to Cry Out to God for Help

There are times during a fast that you just cannot do it on your own. It doesn't matter how much willpower you think you have. You need the help that only the Holy Spirit can give. This is one of the main benefits of fasting. You draw close to God, and you are reminded by your hunger throughout the day how much you need him.

It Gives Your Prayers a Boost

The disciples were trying to cast a demon out of a boy and were having a tough time. Jesus came down and did it without a problem. Later, the disciples went to him and asked why they couldn't do it. He told them in Mark 9:29, "This kind only comes out by prayer and fasting." There may be some things in your life or the lives of the people around you that need that extra boost. Just as you enjoy seasons of fun and pleasure on the outside, be sure to incorporate seasons of fasting as well.

Tips for Family and Friends

Tip #1 – Don't underestimate the effect your prayers have on the life of the released prisoner.

The story of Bolette Hinderli shows us the power of prayer. This young girl took possession of Lars Skrefsrud and made him her unique project. This kind of prayer takes perseverance, and Jesus gives us the perfect example in Luke 18:2-7.

> "In a certain city there was a judge who neither feared God nor respected man. And there was a widow in that city who kept coming to him and saying, 'Give me justice against my adversary.' For a while he refused, but afterward he said to himself, 'Though I neither fear God nor respect man, yet because this widow keeps bothering me, I will give her justice, so that she will not beat me down by her continual coming.'" And the Lord said, "Hear what the unrighteous judge says. And will not God give justice to his elect, who cry to him day and night? Will he delay long over them?"

Don't give up interceding for your lost relative or friend. As long as they still have breath, they are not beyond God's reach. Once they've been released, pray the Lord gives them the strength they need to face the challenges of the day. Pray that God will send angels to surround them and battle on their behalf.

Tip #2 – Consider giving your loved one the gift of a study Bible.

One of the greatest gifts you can give someone is the Word of God. Most prisoners have the option of receiving a free Bible from the chaplain while they are incarcerated. Usually, these Bibles are cheaply produced paperback versions. I was gifted a beautiful leather-bound New International Version Study Bible when I hit the streets. It helped me dig deeper into the Scriptures, and after 26 years, it is still in my possession, even though it is tattered and worn.

Questions for Discussion

1. One theologian said that Christians are like tires. We leak over time and need to be refilled. Why is repetition so important?

2. Why is going into battle without proper training so dangerous?

3. What is your current devotional life like? Do you read the Bible every day? What are some of the benefits of doing this?

4. Do you have anyone who has made you their unique prayer project? How have their prayers impacted you in your Christian life?

5. Why do you think God wants us to pray even though he knows everything we are going through?

6. What is the longest you have ever fasted? Describe your personal experience.

7. What are some of the spiritual dangers Jesus speaks of regarding fasting?

Part III

Life Skills

Get a Job

"For even when we were with you, we would give you this
command: If anyone is not willing to work, let him not eat."
1 Thessalonians 3:10

"We often miss opportunity because
it's dressed in overalls and looks like work."
Thomas A. Edison

I stood around after a seminary class I was teaching in a Soledad (California) prison when a student walked up to me and began talking about his plans for getting a job when he got out.

"I'm not going to tell anyone that I was in prison because I don't want them to judge my ability to work based on my criminal record."

I looked at him, dumbfounded. "You mean you're going to lie about your background to secure a job?"

He responded defensively, "I wouldn't call it lying. I'm just not going to tell them everything about me."

Lying to secure employment is a prevalent mistake for ex-offenders to make. Failing to be truthful about their storied past can actually create more problems in the future. I encouraged the student to reconsider his approach and to tell the truth about his crimes; then I went on to explain my story to the student.

I was honest about my history from the beginning. The first place I applied for a job was a local grocery store, Lunds, in South Minneapolis. On the application, it asked me if I had ever committed a crime. I wrote, "I would like to discuss this in person." A few days after I turned the application into the manager, the store called me and asked if I could come in for an interview. I dressed in casual but business-appropriate clothing, rehearsed in my mind what I wanted to say, and arrived 10 minutes early for the meeting.

The supervisor called me into his office, which ironically doubled as the video surveillance room to catch shoplifters. At the very beginning of our conversation, I told him I had just been released from prison eight days ago. I explained my criminal history to the manager and how the Lord had changed me in jail. I told him about the work I had done in prison and provided references for the bosses I had in the barbershop, upholstery department, and cleaning crew during my incarceration. He took it all in, asked me a few questions, and then talked for a moment about how he felt everyone needed a second chance. Without further consideration, he offered me the job on the spot.

The next day, I started work in the produce department making $8.50 an hour, which was ten times the amount I had made on the inside. I was so glad I had taken the honest route. By telling the truth about your record, you may not get hired like I did, but don't let this deter you. Know that your approach is pleasing to the Lord, who commands us to not bear false witness.

You Can't be Picky

Unless you were able to get some specific vocational training in prison, you might need to take a minimum wage job doing menial work at first. I would recommend you start looking for a job the second or third day after your release. Treat your job search like you would a full-time job. Even before you get out, it's smart to get started on your résumé. Most prisons have career counselors that can help you think through the process and support you in your strategy. The first two jobs I had when I got out were not what I wanted to be doing for the rest of my life. The produce job was part-time, so while I worked at Lunds, I was on the hunt for something full-time as well.

My parole officer told me about a job posting he saw for a pie factory in the suburbs. I decided to give it a try and went through the same interview process that I had at the grocery store. Again, I found the manager was very willing to give me a chance to prove myself. He hired me, and I started the next week working the night shift from 4 pm-2 am.

Pies Incorporated is definitely on the top five list of hardest jobs I've ever had. For ten hours a day, four days a week, I stood next to a conveyor belt with empty pie shells flying by at a rate of one every three seconds. My job was to scoop frozen fruit from a huge steel vat, measure the weight of the fruit and then flip it into the pie shell, trying not to spill any in the process. It was mind-numbing work, and my hands were usually stiff from the frozen blueberries or strawberries within about ten minutes of starting my shift.

This job was a real motivation for me to find something better. I had attended barber school while in prison but just needed to pass my boards on the outside before I could start cutting hair for employment. I studied hard because I didn't want to work any longer than I had to at Pies Inc. Upon my release, I contacted the barber college in Minneapolis and asked them if I could attend some of their refresher classes and practice haircuts at the school. They obliged, and every spare minute I had was spent getting ready for my state exam, even though I was exhausted from my ten-hour shift.

For you, it might mean finishing your education or getting some vocational training. Unless you want to work a minimum wage job for the rest of your life, you will need to sacrifice your free time and work towards a degree. There are many resources available to those getting out of prison to help them discover a meaningful career.

Scriptural Admonition Regarding Work

Most of us had chores when we were children. Chores are an essential part of a family running smoothly. We can also see there are chores to do in the family of God. The Apostle Paul gave this command in 2 Thessalonians 3:10: "For even when we were with you, we would give you this command: If anyone is not willing to work, let him not eat. For we hear that some among you walk in idleness, not busy at work, but busybodies. Now such persons we command and encourage in the Lord Jesus Christ to do their work quietly and to earn their own living."

First, note that Paul instructs Christians, not unbelievers. There have been times when I was parked at a stoplight and saw a homeless man standing with a sign asking for food and this verse would go through my mind as I thought his hunger should be driving him to find a job. But we must recognize that, like most commands in the Bible, believers are the focus. This command speaks to those that have the Spirit of Jesus Christ living and working in them to sanctify them.

Paul states that when he was last with them, he noticed some of them were not working. He had heard a report that some of them were walking in idleness, possibly for the main reason Paul wrote the letter in the first place—some of them thought the return of Jesus already happened. Maybe they were disheartened and felt all was hopeless because they were left behind.

Another reason those attending the church in Thessalonica might have avoided work was because they were only acting as brothers, taking advantage of the Christian goodwill of those working hard. They were not there to be a part of the Body but as parasites. Although we cannot determine if indeed they were Christians or not, Paul warned them about their behavior, and if they did not change they were asked to leave.

Before we move on to the next point, I want you to notice that Paul did not say if you don't work, you don't eat. He said he who was not *willing* to work should not eat. There are many out there who are eager to work, but for whatever reason, they cannot. They may be too sick, or they may not be able to find a job because of the economy. That is where the church can step in to help.

The second reason God gives His people the command to work is because being idle leads to a chaotic life. Lack of work creates disorder. There is an old saying I think proves very true. "Idle hands are the devil's workshop." At the church in Thessalonica, this was the case. Those who were not busy at work were meddling in other people's lives and stirring up dissension because they didn't have anything better to do.

When I was in prison, I loved to work. Whenever there was a lockdown, I would go crazy in my cell left alone with hours of free time and only books to keep me company. Even in the case of those who decide to retire, they must remain actively working at something, whether it is some form of charitable work or a hobby that keeps them busy. At the very least, they don't end up driving their wives or husbands insane by pacing around the house all day.

Another way idleness causes disorder is in the neglect of duties. Perhaps you have a job, but you know you are not working at it as you should. Maybe you have cut corners and given Christianity a bad name by your shoddy work. Diligence is especially crucial in jobs where there is no immediate supervision. I know for myself it's necessary to keep looking back over my list of tasks that I need to be working on not to be led into time-wasting diversions.

Notice how the Bible describes the one who is following the Lord's command to work—they do so in quietness. They are not creating a disturbance. There is something beautiful about a man or woman who goes quietly about their business giving glory to God for the talents he has given them. Whether they receive fame or their lives go completely unnoticed by society does not matter. They work for an audience of One.

Ephesians 4:28 shows us the reason we do this work. "Let the thief no longer steal, but rather let him labor, doing honest work with his own hands, so that he may have something to share with anyone in need." I was a thief for years. When I became a Christian, I left that life behind me. I now provide for my family by doing honest work. In addition, according to Paul's command, the money I make is supposed to assist in the church's work of helping the poor.

Consider the following illustration. A horse and a cart are trying to make it up a very steep hill. There are those onboard that jump off and help push. Some stay on the wagon and cheer for the horse and pushers, while others drag their feet. The type of people we are is evident in the work we do. Are we pushers, riders, or foot draggers?

Historical legend says that as a carpenter, Jesus made the best oxen yokes in the world. People would come from miles around to buy them.[ix] As we represent Jesus, our work should make the Christian message attractive. There is a story of a man who was negotiating a house without even looking at it. His friend asked him why he wasn't concerned he would show up and find things were not as promised. He replied, "I know the man who built the house, so I know the house will be sound." Can people say that about your work?

The Perks of Owning a Business

After about three months at Pies Incorporated, I passed my barber boards and was grateful to work at Dick's Sport's Barbers in Minneapolis for six years. Dick was a kind and generous boss. I wanted to make the most of the chance he had given me as an ex-con, so I worked hard. However, though I loved his shop and the six other barbers I worked alongside, I knew I would not be there for the rest of my career. I wanted to open my own place. I had ideas about how a barbershop should operate, and I couldn't shake that dream.

I spoke to my grandpa about this dream, and he was very supportive of my ideas. I began to look around for shops that were for sale, but for several months didn't find the right fit. That was until I walked into Fremont Barbers and met Jim Rust. He had owned his shop in North Minneapolis for 43 years, and at age 72 wanted to semi-retire. We sat and talked for about an hour, and later that week, my grandpa stopped by to check the place out. Jim and I negotiated a deal, and on January 1, 2000, I became only the third owner of Fremont Barbers in its 75-year history.

Being a business owner for 12 years taught me some valuable lessons. First, I learned it's best to take over an existing shop rather than start one from scratch. Jim had worked diligently during his career to build a good reputation in the neighborhood. Everyone knew him there, and most of those clients were willing to give me a chance based on his recommendation. Jim stayed on working part-time when I took over; he didn't want to fully retire because that little shop had become the center of his world. The main reason he sold it to me was he didn't want to have to deal with the financial side any longer.

I would have probably made more money if I had purchased the shop under the stipulation that Jim had to retire fully. The majority of his patrons would have given me a shot as their new barber, and that would have been direct income in my pocket. The reason I didn't do this was not some brilliant business decision on my part. I did it because of Jesus' golden rule: "Do unto others as you would have them do unto you." I knew if I was in Jim's position, I would want someone to let me work as long as possible. Karma is not a real thing, unlike God blessing you for doing the right thing. The Lord truly blessed me by giving me a mentor and friend in Jim.

The second lesson I learned was not to waste my money on advertising. I had this supposedly great idea when I first took over Fremont Barbers. I decided to make up a bunch of flyers with a $5 off coupon for first-time customers. I printed hundreds of them and spent hours walking around the neighborhood, hanging them on people's front doors and slipping them under the windshield wipers of cars. To my dismay, I had only one person come to the shop with a coupon. After this failed advertising campaign, I asked Jim why it didn't work. He said, "Your haircuts are your best billboard. If you do a good job for your customers, word will get around." The only advertising I did after that was to pay to have our shop's name in a local high-school basketball game program, and the only reason I did it was because it was a customer who approached me.

The third thing I learned as a small business owner was that God would provide. Barbering is a lot like farming; you don't know from year to year if you are going to make it or not. Some months I felt like I had made the best business decision in the world because we had extra money for family outings and home improvements. Other months I didn't know if I was going to be able to pay our mortgage. At the time, my wife, Mary, was homeschooling the kids and our only source of income was from the shop. I prayed constantly during those years, and God never let me down. There always seemed to be money available when we needed it. We were not wealthy by any stretch of the imagination, but we were content and happy as a family.

I don't want anyone to think that working for someone else is somehow second-best. Owning a small business is not for everyone. For my friend Jordan, starting his own landscaping company was a necessity. Even though he was upfront and honest with potential employers about his crimes, he couldn't seem to catch a break. After months of looking, he decided to start his own corporation, and now all of his employees are ex-offenders. If you find it challenging to secure a job when you get out, it may be that God is nudging you in the direction of starting something new, and remember, when the Lord guides, he provides.

Work in Heaven

Some people think that when they go to heaven, they will be sitting on a white cloud, strumming a harp all day. I don't know about you, but that seems pretty dull to me. Others believe they will be playing golf all the time and think of heaven as an extended vacation. I love golf more than most people I know, but the thought of playing endless rounds for thousands of years seems pretty meaningless, not to mention, selfish.

One of the first things God did after creating Adam and Eve in the Garden of Eden was to put them to work. In Genesis 1:28, he said, "Be fruitful and increase in number; fill the earth and subdue it. Rule over the fish in the sea and the birds in the sky and over every living creature that moves on the ground." The earth needed subduing. It was not Disneyland, but rather, it was wild and untamed. Adam and Eve's job was to tend it.

> One of the first things God did after creating humans was put them to work.

There are specific jobs that will be obsolete in heaven. With the absence of sickness, sin, and death, doctors, lawyers, and correctional officers will need to find new employment. But who's to say there will not be work in heaven. Jesus seemed to indicate there will be even greater and more significant tasks there. Consider Luke 19:17 in which he stated, "And he said to him, 'Well done, good servant! Because you have been faithful a very little, you shall have authority over ten cities.'" As a faithful steward of Fremont Barbers, perhaps I will be given authority over the heavenly barber's guild. I've always wanted to serve Jesus by trimming his beard.

Working hard in this life not only helps you succeed and provide for your family, but it also catches the attention of our Heavenly Father. I pray you will hear his words, "Well done, good and faithful servant!"

Tips for Family and Friends

Tip #1 – Don't Let Your Loved One Freeload

There may be a short period right when a prisoner gets out that they will need financial support from family and friends. Notice I said a *short* period. If they move into your home, set a realistic deadline for them to begin their job search. They will probably need to look at options nearby at first because most ex-offenders' drivers licenses have lapsed. If you have the time, you may decide to drive them to interviews, but at some point, they will need to begin to use public transportation to get to their job.

If you decide to give your loved one money, DON'T LOAN IT TO THEM! Instead, make it a gift. Proverbs 22:7 says, "The rich rules over the poor, and the borrower is the slave of the lender." You are part of their support team, not their slave-master. When they get back on their feet, they may choose to reimburse you for the money, but don't expect it. That will only create tension in your relationship.

Tip #2 – Help the Ex-offender Dream Big

One of the critical issues for those who have committed crimes and have spent years in prison is the lack of self-esteem. If they are now Christians, they will experience a significant amount of remorse for the things they have done. Memories of their past may cause them to feel like they don't deserve to live "the good life." They think the punishment needs to continue even after they have paid their debt to society. That is a lie straight from the pit of hell!

Even though they have made some serious mistakes, they can go on to overcome them. They can still achieve the dreams they had when they were a child. When I got out of prison, I was 25 years old. Most of the people I went to high school with had already started their careers. Many of them were married and had begun to have children. I felt like I had a lot of catching up to do. Those who were in my support group made sure I realized that I still had plenty of time to get my life back on track. You can be that voice of reason for your son, daughter, or friend.

GET OUT FOR GOOD

Questions for Discussion

1. Do you plan to be honest with future employers about your criminal past? How will you convince them you have changed? Practice a mock interview with another group member right now.

2. Have you received any vocational training in prison? What are the steps you will need to take on the outside to secure a job in that field?

3. How do you feel about using public transportation, and what are your goals for getting your license back?

4. What were some of the dreams you had as a child that you feel might be unattainable upon your release? Why do you think they are unrealistic?

5. Scott mentioned some jobs that will be obsolete in heaven. Can you think of others that will not exist? What would your dream job be in eternity?

6. Regarding the jobs you have had in prison, do you think the Lord would say, "Well done, good and faithful servant" about your performance in these menial tasks?

7. How much money will you have when you get out? How do you plan to spend it?

10

Buy a House

"But the meek shall inherit the land
and delight themselves in abundant peace."
Psalm 37:11

"He is not a full man who does not own a piece of land."
Hebrew Proverb

I was enjoying life in the Lundin's basement. They were only charging me $250 a month for room and board, which included terrific meals prepared by Sandy. Plus, my responsibilities were pretty minimal; as long as I kept the basement clean and helped with a few household chores, they were happy.

I was making good money at Dick's Sports Barbers, so I had plenty of spare cash to spend on bachelor living. The members of the Kinship Group loved to hang out together, enjoying outings at restaurants, sporting events, theatres, and yes, even bowling. This situation went on for about a year and a half. Then Pete dropped a bombshell on me.

One day, as we were working in the garage, he said, "Scott, I'm proud of the progress you've made in your maturity toward Christian manhood. I think the next step in your growth is to buy a house." BOOM! I almost dropped the wrench I was holding. I gawked at him with my mouth gaping. He continued, "A man needs to own a piece of real-estate. It firmly plants him in the community and adds stability to his life. He begins to use his excess cash-flow to build equity instead of wasting it on continuous pleasure." I'm sure I blushed a bit at this last bit. He recognized that I'd overfilled my calendar with "fun" events. He had kept quiet about it for a long time, but sensed the time was right to take another step in the journey.

Up until that moment, I had a renter's mentality. Throughout my entire adult life, I had depended on others to provide shelter for me. The army housed me in the barracks, numerous others had rented rooms out to me, and the government provided me with a six by eight-foot cell during my incarceration. Now, I was content and enjoying my cozy apartment in Pete and Sandy's finished basement, but owning a house seemed to be beyond my capability. In addition, I had a very negative attitude toward home-ownership based on my childhood.

When I was in fifth grade, my mom and step-dad, Charlie, announced to the family that we were going to build a house. My step-dad's father had given him a small plot of land between a cornfield and a cow pasture about eight miles from Boyd, Wisconsin, population 635. We were finally going to fulfill my mom's dream to build her "little house on the prairie." We moved out of the house we were renting and relocated to a tent on the new property. I was excited! When you're ten years old, living in a tent and watching the construction process unfold is highly entertaining.

The excitement factor wore off quickly. Things progressed slowly that humid summer, but thankfully by the time the winter snow came, the basement was finished and capped with a temporary tar-paper roof, and we moved in, all ten of us. I think things would have been fine if it wasn't for the fact my mom and stepdad constantly fought during the construction process. They each had a different philosophy about money. My mom wanted to take out a loan and finish the entire house within a year whereas Charlie wanted to build as they had the extra cash, which was scarce. This disagreement created a significant amount of tension in that 400 square foot hole in the ground.

I was relieved when, after about six months, my mom got fed up with the conflict and we ran off to stay with my grandparents, once again, dependent on someone else for shelter. My step-dad succeeded in convincing my mom he was going to make real progress on the house. The second section of the four-part split level had been framed and covered with tar-paper, and we made the journey from Minneapolis back to Boyd. This cycle happened about half a dozen times over the next six years. We would run away, Charlie would add a bit more onto the house, and we would move back in. Each time we did, my loathing of homeownership increased. Eventually, their relational troubles increased to the point where my mom and step-dad divorced. To this day, that little house on the prairie sits unfinished, a constant reminder of how not to do homeownership.

There Comes a Time to Stop Freeloading

When you get out of prison, you will need a place to stay. For some of you, that will come in the form of transitional housing through a ministry or government agency. For others, a family member or friend will offer shelter in their home. Whatever situation you find yourself in, the main thing to remember is this situation is supposed to be temporary. By temporary, I mean less than a couple of years. Under exceptional circumstances, this transition may take longer, but for most, it should only be as long as it takes you to get back on your feet. As soon as you are released, it's crucial to start setting aside a portion of your paycheck toward a down payment for a house.

Like me, most ex-offenders will have a list of experiences they want to take part in when they get out from behind bars. We keep a mental checklist of all the activities we've missed out on while we were incarcerated. During the time I was locked up, they started building the Mall of America and so that became one of the places I had on my checklist. I wanted to go shopping there with my family so I could get some new clothes, try out the different restaurants, and enjoy the rides at the indoor theme park. I also had hopes of traveling and went on a short-term mission trip to Belize within the first year of my release. I encourage you to have fun when you get out (See Chapter 11) but realize that your checklist is going to cost money. Pleasure is expensive. Set a limit on the percentage of your income that will go toward fulfilling your experiential goals.

> **Most prisoners have a list of things they want to do when they get out.**

In the process of enjoying your newfound freedom, strive for independence. This attitude can be difficult for someone who has been dependent upon the state or federal system for years or even decades. Having every decision made for you from what you will eat to where you will work can create psychological problems. Inmates start to feel like our destinies are beyond our control. We get the idea that we cannot achieve the same goals that ordinary people on the outside can. We may even believe homeownership is beyond our grasp.

The Bible Speaks of Home Ownership

The first thing we must recognize when we look at biblical passages that describe real estate is most of them are addressed to the people of Israel, thus, they might not directly apply to the modern Christian. You are not literally making the transition from an Egyptian slave to a property owner in the Promised Land. Keeping that in mind, we can still find general principles that are relevant to today's context.

The Lord Desires to Bless You

Moses was on a mission from God. He was to go down to Egypt and free Israel from its captivity. Once released, what was their final destination? Exodus 3:17 calls it "a land flowing with milk and honey." Milk indicated it had lush pastures for cattle, while honey suggested there were fruit trees and flowers everywhere. Wouldn't it have been strange if God had told them, "I am leading you to a land of disease, famine, and starvation."? How many of them do you think would have chosen to stay behind in Egypt where at least they had food?

When God leads you out of your captivity, he is not going to let you starve. He's not leading you into failure. Consider Jerimiah 29:11, which states, "For I know the plans I have for you, declares the Lord, plans for welfare and not for evil, to give you a future and a hope." Your 'Promised Land' is a place of blessing and life, and the Lord will ensure your survival on the outside. That doesn't mean it won't come without its challenges. When the Israelites were preparing to enter the land God had promised them, the Lord commanded them to send out 12 spies to scout it out and bring back a report. When they returned after 40 days to give their account, the spies were experiencing a mix of emotions.

On one hand, they were excited the land's produce was just as God had promised. It was flowing with milk and honey, as indicated by the luscious sample of fruit they brought with them. But it also contained giants. They told Joshua, "However, the people who dwell in the land are strong, and the cities are fortified and very large. And besides, we saw the descendants of Anak there" (Numbers 13:28). They go on, in verse 33, to tell the people, "We seemed to ourselves like grasshoppers, and so we seemed to them."

You will face some giants as you begin your new life on the outside. Don't be like the people of Israel who, in fear, refused to take them on, and instead of taking position of the land, they wandered in the wilderness for 40 years. God will help you overcome any obstacle, no matter how fortified it seems.

Some of the giants you will face may be things like inadequate job skills to secure a high-paying salary, lack of family support, or insufficient real estate experience. Even though you may be deficient in these areas, remember what you do have; just like the Israelites, you have the presence of God.

Moses was speaking to the Lord one day and had a bit of an argument with him. God told him he was going to send an angel ahead of them into the land. Moses countered by saying, "If your presence will not go with me, do not bring us up from here" (Exodus 33:15). It was easy for Moses to know where God's presence was leading him because he had a cloud to follow by day and a pillar of fire to follow by night. It will be a bit more difficult for you.

You will need to spend time seeking the Lord with prayer and fasting regarding the next step you are to take. It will come like a still, small voice; only a whisper. "Whether you turn to the right or to the left, your ears will hear a voice behind you, saying, 'This is the way; walk in it'" (Isaiah 30:21). He didn't bring you this far to abandon you in the wilderness. Confidently go forward knowing he will never leave you or forsake you.

You Must Prepare for Homeownership

The book of Proverbs contains nuggets of wisdom Solomon left for his sons. He knew a thing or two about being a property owner because he was the wealthiest king that ever ruled over Israel. In Proverbs 24:27, he advised, "Prepare your work outside; get everything ready for yourself in the field, and after that, build your house." Essentially, he was saying to make sure you have an adequate income before you pull the trigger on buying a house.

While I was running my barbershop, I decided to get my realtor's license. I wanted to earn some extra income by helping my shop clients and was looking to purchase a rental property. In real estate school, I learned the typical down payment for a house is somewhere between 10–20 percent of the list price of the house. For example, if you are looking to purchase a home that is $300,000, you will want to save between $30–$60 thousand to have an adequate down payment.

There are exceptions to this rule. If you are a veteran, like me, you can apply for a one-time VA loan. These loans typically have a lower interest rate than other mortgage lenders offer, and you do not have to pay anything down unless you choose to, as it is not required. Besides, credit rating qualifications are less stringent. To qualify, you must meet one of the following criteria:

- Served 90 consecutive days of active service during wartime;
- Served 181 days of active service during peacetime;
- Be an active member of the National Guard or Reserves for six years or more; or
- Have been married to a service member who died in the line of duty or as a result of a service-related disability.

At the closing, you will pay a one-time fee. If you decide not to put any money down, that fee is 2.15% of the purchase price. If you put at least 10% down, your fee drops to 1.25%. One of the greatest benefits of having a VA loan is you are not required to pay private mortgage insurance, an expense that can increase your monthly payment by $100 or more.

Even if you are not a veteran, you'll find programs for first-time homebuyers that can significantly reduce the down payment you are required to bring to the table. There are federal and state programs, so set up a meeting with a trusted mortgage company to find out your qualifications. If you don't know any mortgage lenders, talk to people in your church about contacting a real estate agent; almost everyone knows at least one realtor. This meeting will not cost you anything because agents representing buyers earn money from commissions (paid for by the seller) they split with the seller's agent during the sale of a home. In California, the state I live in, there are currently 14 different programs for first-time homebuyers, some of which are offered to those with low credit scores. Your agent will put you in touch with a mortgage broker.

As soon as you get out of prison, begin saving money for your down payment. I would recommend an initial amount of 10% of your take-home pay. If you are clearing $50,000 a year, you will have at least $25,000 in five years, plus any interest that money earns. In most markets that should be enough to get you a starter home. I know five years might seem like a long time to wait to make a purchase, but time on the outside goes by much more quickly than on the inside. Remember, the time is going to pass by whether you save or not, so make the most of your employment by setting aside a nest egg for the future.

The point is you can do this. It's not an impossible dream! With hard work and patience, you can become a property owner. I have seen many ex-cons do it. Solomon points to a tiny insect as an example of what you can accomplish with a little diligence. "Go to the ant, you sluggard; consider its ways and be wise! It has no commander, no overseer or ruler, yet it stores its provisions in summer and gathers its food at harvest" (Proverbs 6:6-8).

Choose a Home Within Your Means

In 1991, H. Jackson Brown Jr. wrote a devotional self-help book entitled *Life's Little Instruction Book*. He wrote it for his son as he left for college to offer him insights, straightforward suggestions, and heartfelt humor about how to face the challenges of life. Since its initial publication, it has sold more than 10 million copies and has been translated into 33 different languages. In the book, he gives some great advice regarding homeownership. Tip #17 is "Live within your means," and tip #18 is "Drive inexpensive cars, but own the best house you can afford."[x] Buying a home within your means doesn't mean you need to buy a dump. It means you need to determine what you can afford over the term of the loan.

Most mortgages today are 30-year fixed-rate loans. You will be making that house payment for a good chunk of your adult life unless you happen to inherit tons of money from a wealthy family member. Choosing wisely on the front end of the purchase will ensure you don't end up house-poor.

Jesus told a parable about a foolish chap who didn't heed this advice regarding his building project. "For which of you, desiring to build a tower, does not first sit down and count the cost, whether he has enough to complete it? Otherwise, when he has laid a foundation and is not able to finish, all who see it begin to mock him, saying, 'This man began to build and was not able to finish'" (Luke 14:28–30). His main point was about discipleship, not real estate, but the example still fits our context.

Foreclosure is not fun. This catastrophe occurs when you discover you have purchased a home beyond your means and are not able to make the mortgage payments. Foreclosures in the U.S. reached an all-time high in the third quarter of 2009. The reason for this was greed. Property values had increased at an alarming rate in the previous decade, and even though almost everyone predicted a crash, most mortgage companies didn't reign in their lending practices. They were making boatloads of money from refinancing fees by allowing refinances for things like debt consolidation, family vacations, and auto purchases. When market values began to plummet, many found they owed more on their house than it was worth and had drained all their equity through the refinancing process. When they went to try to sell their home, they faced what is called a short sale. They had to write a check at the closing to cover the portion of the loan the transaction didn't cover. Buying within your means will help you avoid this problem.

As you sit down to figure out how much you can afford on a home purchase, consider the following:

- Consumerreports.org suggests you limit your mortgage payment to under 25% of your after-tax income. Currently, our mortgage

GET OUT FOR GOOD

is 20% of our take-home pay. As a Christian who tithes, you may find this more reasonable.

- Over time, your wage should increase. Even though you may initially find you're getting closer to that 25% boundary than you would like, salary raises will begin to give you a bit more breathing room the older you get.

- The longer you stay in a home, the better. The industry rule of thumb is to remain in your house for at least five years. In a typical market, you will begin to create serious equity after this benchmark.

- Take into consideration the condition of the home you are purchasing. If it hasn't been updated in the last 15 years, you will need to set aside extra money for home improvements. Appliances will break down, roofs will leak, and you will need to upgrade your furnace at some point. If you live below your means, you will have the necessary funds to cover these expenses.

The Importance of Upkeep

Purchasing a home will probably be the biggest investment you make in your life. The equity you build over the course of the loan can be significant. Let's say you bought a house for $250,000 and owned it for ten years before you decided to sell it. According to the Global Property Guide, homes have increased about 45% in the United States over the last decade. That means your $250,000 house would be worth about $360,000. You've increased your equity by $110,000. However, you must take into consideration that as the seller, there are fees you will need to pay at closing, which Zillow.com estimates these costs at between 8% to 10%. On the high side, you will need to pay fees in the amount of $36,000, which reduces your equity to $74,000.

Another factor to consider is that as the owner of the home, you have to pay for all the upkeep a landlord would typically cover if you were renting. This includes the maintenance of the home as well as any remodeling you've done. Let's just say for the sake of argument that you've incurred maintenance costs of $5,000 a year, which is a high estimate. That would reduce your equity at closing to $24,000. That means in the ten years you've lived in your home, you have earned about $200 a month. That's not a bad return!

To make the most of your investment, you need to preserve the condition of the home. You can't just let it fall apart around you and think you are still going to get top dollar when you sell it. I've owned three different homes in the last 26 years, and have made significant improvements in each of them. Three areas that most improve the value are bathrooms, kitchens, and landscaping (which increases curb appeal). Make sure you factor into your monthly budget money to make improvements to your house.

Homeownership is a fantastic adventure. It helps you stay grounded, gives added purpose to your life, and increases responsibility; these three essential elements help keep your feet on the straight and narrow.

Tips for Family and Friends

Tip #1 – You can give a gift to your loved one to help with a down payment.

Coming up with a down payment for a house is a big challenge. You may want to give your child or friend a helping hand in this area. According to thebalance.com, in 2018, the IRS allows you to give a gift of up to $30,000 towards a down payment without being hit with a gift tax. The money will need to be transferred into their account early into the mortgage process because mortgage lenders want to see the funds are available to them. Remember, legally, this cannot be a loan; it's a gift that should not be expected to be paid back.

Each mortgage company's underwriting department has different rules as to how they handle gift monies. Talk with your mortgage lender beforehand to see if a one-time gift is the best fit for you.

Tip #2 – Make yourself available during the home selection process.

When I lived in Minneapolis, we had some friends that were in the process of purchasing a home. They had already been approved for the financing and had narrowed their search to a darling split level in the suburbs. The last step was to have the inspection done. They invited us to come for the walk-through with them to see what we thought.

Everything looked great until we went down into the basement. The inspector began to move some boxes and a ping pong table, which was along one of the walls. By moving the table, he discovered about the worst thing you could in the realm of home inspections. A huge crack was running from the upper corner of the wall down to the bottom of the foundation. You could look through the crack and see dirt on the other side of the block. Needless to say, that discovery was a deal killer. Our friends knew it would probably cost over $100 thousand to replace the basement wall and foundation of that house. They couldn't ignore it because a series of other problems would ensue if it wasn't fixed.

Proverbs 15:22 states, "Without counsel plans fail, but with many advisers, they succeed." The home buying process can be intoxicating for someone that has never owned a house. You can provide an objective opinion about issues that may create future problems leading to buyers' remorse.

Questions for Discussion

1. Did your family rent or own when you were a kid? What was your impression of this living situation?

2. Do you feel like homeownership is something you can accomplish? Why or why not?

3. Why is achieving independence so important to Christian growth?

4. What are some practical steps you can take to ensure that you will set aside a portion of your income towards a down payment?

5. Talk about your dream home. Where would it be located? What kinds of amenities would you like it to have?

6. How does the purchasing and lending process make you feel? Why?

7. Are you handy when it comes to fixing things? What will your approach be to home maintenance once you make a purchase?

Have Some Fun

"A joyful heart is good medicine,
but a crushed spirit dries up the bones."
Proverbs 17:22

"Thank you, Lord, for giving us baseball.
It shows us that you like us."
Trinity High School Coach Grant Combs

One of the attributes my stepdad, Charlie, instilled in me was a solid work ethic. The necessity for this came from the fact we were probably hovering near the poverty line my entire childhood. Charlie worked in a paper mill in rural Wisconsin that would seasonally lay off its employees, often for three or four months at a time. To supplement his income, we cut and sold firewood to the local farmers. Every weekend during the school year and every day during the summer, I would hear the tractor start up out on the gravel driveway. That was the signal to wake up, get dressed, grab some toast, and jump on the wood trailer.

For some odd reason, our house was the first stop for the school bus in the morning and the last stop at night, which meant I had an hour-long ride each way in which to get all my school work done. I needed to do this because I knew when I got home around 4:30, there would be an enormous pile of wood to stack waiting for me atop the icy wind-swept hill near our house. My brother and I would work until dinner, eat, do the dishes, watch an hour of TV and head to bed.

During those years in the woods, my body grew strong, and my shoulders broadened significantly. I was a skinny kid in elementary school, but by the time I turned sixteen, I was driving the tractor, running a chainsaw, splitting elm logs, and grabbing a sizeable chunk of wood in each hand to throw 20 feet onto the trailer. I grew to my maximum adult height of six-foot over the summer between my sophomore and junior year in high school. When the wrestling coach saw me walking down the hall the first week of school, he stopped me and said, "Stroud, how much do you weigh?" I told him we didn't have a scale at home, but I thought I was about 175 pounds. He smiled and said, "Perfect! Would you be willing to stop by the locker room during lunch and let me weigh you?" I told him the only wrestling I'd done was with my brother on the grass in our front yard. "Don't worry about it," he responded. "We'll get you trained in."

The thought of joining the wrestling squad filled me with excitement. I had never been that great at sports, even though my mom had taught me to throw and hit a softball. I met with coach LaFlamme before lunch, and he had me strip down to my underwear and step on the scale in the deserted locker room. He adjusted the metal slide to the correct position and announced the results, "172!" He gave my wiry, farmer-tanned arms a look and said, "I have an open position at 167 this season. Do you think you could make that weight by the time practices start in October?" I told him I would have to ask my folks.

I brought up the subject that evening at dinner, and the reaction was less than encouraging. My mom's biggest concern was how I was going to get home since we lived in the country twelve miles from where the school was in Stanley. I told her there was a sports bus that would drop me off. She nodded and smiled at me, so I knew I'd cleared that hurdle. I hadn't yet heard any comment from Charlie's direction. Looking down at his mashed potatoes, he said, "What about your chores?" I knew that was coming, so I replied, "I can stack wood when I get home from wrestling." A conflicted look clouded his rugged features, and I could tell he was struggling with the idea.

My stepdad had never played sports in high school, and we never watched sports on TV. For him, growing up on a dairy farm in a family of 15, there was no time for extra-curricular activities. He looked up at me after a few moments of thought and said, "As long as it doesn't interfere with your work, you can wrestle." Although he never attended any of my meets, I think Charlie instinctively knew I needed this. He had an athletic build, and I wondered if he regretted not being able to play football when he attended Stanley High School. I know he had the genetics because his son from his first marriage, Joe, grew to 6'4" and 220 pounds and was a fantastic tight end in college. To this day, Joe competes in ironman triathlons around the country.

All Work and No Play

There is an interesting verse in Zechariah chapter eight. The prophet is describing what the conditions of Jerusalem would be when God restored the people of Israel after their Babylonian captivity. Verse five says, "And the streets of the city shall be full of boys and girls playing in its streets." One of the indicators of God's protective blessing seems to be children at play. In a healthy, godly society, we should see kids joyfully and freely engaging in recreation in our neighborhoods. Beyond this, we should also see adults taking time to enjoy life by taking time to play. As was mentioned in chapter five, there is a season for everything. Included in the list of seasons, Solomon states there is a time to laugh and a time to dance. When you get out of prison, you must include plenty of laughing and dancing in your schedule.

Some have taken 1 Corinthians 13:11 and misapplied it to all aspects of life. It says, "When I was a child, I spoke like a child, I thought like a child, I reasoned like a child. When I became a man, I gave up childish ways." Paul is specifically talking about our thought process. We should not be naïve like children being tossed here and there by every new doctrine we hear (see Ephesians 4:14). But obviously, Jesus thought very highly of being childlike in certain aspects of life because he said in Matthew 18:4, "Whoever humbles himself like this child is the greatest in the kingdom of heaven."

> Jesus thought highly of being like a child in certain aspects.

To what was Jesus referring? He was specifically talking about their humility. I see eight main ways that children are humble.

1. Children are dependent upon their guardians.
2. Children are weak and not afraid to admit they cannot do something.
3. Children let their emotions out.
4. Children seek out love and the things they need.
5. Children don't have prejudices.
6. Little children are not worried about what people think.

7. Children are very trusting and innocent.
8. They will play with a cardboard box if that's all they have.

Erik Thoennes, in his article entitled, "Created to Play: Thoughts on Play, Sport, and the Christian Life" talks about the importance of this life skill.

> "A Christian who takes his role as a minister seriously must be able to lead people in godly play. As a pastor of a dear flock of growing saints and teacher of college students who generally have a deep hunger to know God, I'm convinced that helping God's people survive in a broken world requires a well-developed ability to play. A minister of the gospel must be able to cry and mourn, laugh, and play with godly gusto, and lead others in these as well."[xi]

After seminary, I received a call from St. Ansgar's Free Lutheran Church in Salinas, California. They wanted me to be their family pastor. I had the privilege of serving under Pastor Herb Hoff for five years up until his retirement. When I arrived on the job, he had been ministering for more than three decades and knew a thing or two about how to survive the stress of pastoral life. After about six months, he told me, "Scott, you're working too hard. You need to take some time for yourself, or you're going to burn out." I had noticed he took regular time away from the rigors of ministry to attend events at the Swiss Rifle Club in Monterey. This hobby helped him "let off some steam."

I knew this was good advice, but was unsure what my hobby should be. One day after Sunday services, I was talking to John

Dick, a member of our congregation, about Herb's advice. John asked me what I would do if money and time were not a factor. I replied, "That's easy. I'd golf, but it's too expensive in this area." He smiled and said, "Maybe not. There is a golf course in the area that offers free memberships for clergy." My jaw dropped! It sounded too good to be accurate, but he insisted I check it out. The next day I called the clubhouse and spoke to the head pro. He said they were still offering the program and encouraged me to write a letter to the general manager. Two weeks later, I received my free membership card in the mail and, thus, rekindled my love for the fantastic game of golf. Virtually every Friday for the past eight years, I've been chasing that elusive white ball around the rolling hills of the Monterey Peninsula.

There are three primary benefits that have come from this habit. First, playing golf has helped me take my mind off of my job. Pastoral life can become all-consuming. It's not like many jobs where you clock out at a specific time, go home, and forget about the tasks you need to accomplish for that day. When I am on the golf course, I am focused on the next shot. Perfecting my golf swing consumes me. I'm trying to beat my previous score and compete with the other guys in my foursome.

Secondly, playing golf gets me out into God's creation. When my wife and I arrived in California for our initial interview with St. Ansgar's, we flew into San Jose airport. Sonja Loftus, the chairperson of the call committee, picked us up in her Jaguar and drove us 60 miles down interstate 101 to Salinas. I looked out at the hills that skirted the highway and was shocked at how dry and dead everything was compared to our home in Minnesota. I commented on this to Sonja, and she said, "Yep, that's why they call it 'Golden California.'" Later that evening, I privately told Mary I didn't think I could live here because of the dead vegetation. She wisely responded, "If it's the Lord, he will give you a love for California."

The next day we drove by some of the renowned golf courses of the Monterey Peninsula: Pebble Beach, Cypress Point, and Pacific Grove Links. The lush and perfectly manicured fairways and greens snuggled up against the rocky shores of the bay, and I was astounded at how beautiful they were. Spending time on these magnificent courses helps me connect with God in nature. The first time I golfed after we moved to California, I stood on the seventh green of Laguna Seca Golf Ranch with tears in my eyes, praising the Lord for moving us here.

Finally, playing golf helps me meet people outside my regular Christian circles. About six months after I received my free membership, I paired up with a couple of other guys for my round, as joining strangers to play happens quite often in golf. That day I met a guy named Ken Ruggerio. Ken had just recently moved from Texas with his wife. He owns a tile business, and golf was his chosen 'escape' as well from the rigors of work. We hit it off immediately. Over the next few months, we ran into each other at the golf course and joined up to play together. A deep friendship began to form.

About a year and a half later, a friend of mine from the Baptist church down the road from our Lutheran church told me they were interviewing a pastor from Arizona named John Bosic. She was the chairperson of their call committee and asked me if I would mind taking Pastor John out to golf. I was more than happy to do so, and when he decided to take the call to Salinas, Ken and I had our third member. Just recently, we've added a fourth regular, Jeff, who grew up a Christian, but had a bad experience in college at a conference, causing him to wander from his faith. He is currently reconsidering his relationship with the Lord because of some conversations we have had while playing.

I would have never met these men if it wasn't for golf. You will find it necessary to break out of your Christian circles so you can meet people in the community. Recreation will help accomplish this goal.

Find Your Type of Fun

Fun is a very subjective concept. Loosely defined, it means enjoyment, amusement, or lighthearted pleasure. Your type of fun may be very different than mine. For instance, my stepdad's idea of entertainment was deer hunting. Before the season started in Wisconsin, we would walk the woods for hours looking for the right spot for a tree stand or a patch of thicket we could drive to scare up the deer. I hated deer hunting season! First off, we would get up about two hours before sunrise so we could get out into the woods by the crack of dawn. This way, we would catch the deer in transition from their night feeding to bedding down for the day.

Secondly, it's freezing in late November, early December, in Wisconsin. We sat there shivering for hours in the first rays of daylight waiting for the elusive whitetail buck to wander by so we could blast him. To this day, I have no desire to go hunting, unless I'm hunting for my golf ball in the bushes after an errant shot.

You need to figure out what fun looks like for you. Don't let anyone tell you what your type of pleasure should be. You may participate in activities you don't enjoy because you love the people you're with, but that's not fun, that's sacrifice. This happens quite often in marriage. As I write this I am sitting in a hotel restaurant in Tucson, Arizona having breakfast. Our church sent me and my wife on a retreat to reenergize after a very busy year. Yesterday, Mary asked me what I wanted to do. I knew the answer she wanted to hear, so I said, "Let's go hiking at the state park." Her eyes lit up, "Really!?"

When I was 21, I severely injured my ankle playing volleyball in prison. It has never been the same, so my idea of hiking is window shopping for half an hour on a flat sidewalk. Mary's ideal hike is a three-hour death march through severe rocky elevation changes. Another factor that detracts from the 'fun' of hiking is that I'm a far cry from the 172 pounds I was during my wrestling years. By the time we hit the top of the first rise during our hike, I was out of breath and had to walk sort of sideways on my bad foot. Mary glanced back and said, "How ya doin'?" I mustered up some enthusiasm, "Fine!" My 'fun' that day was the pleasure of watching Mary in her element.

This kind of sacrifice is needed to navigate relationships in life, but you still need to find your fun activities so you don't burn out. I would recommend something you can do at least once a week. If you find something you like, don't let anyone tell you it's not fun just because they don't see the enjoyment in it. Your idea of a good time might even look like work to them, such as woodworking or gardening. If it rejuvenates you, go for it!

For those of you with children, I would offer a word of caution. Some parents force their children into participating in activities they love, but the children hate. I took my daughter, Cassie, to the driving range when she was eleven. She wanted to go with me, and I thought maybe she had a natural gift for the game. To this day, she is the only person I have ever seen hit a golf ball backward at the practice facility. It appeared golf wasn't her thing, although she did enjoy driving the golf cart around the course that day. As parents, we do need to force our children to get out to try many activities. Otherwise, they would just sit on the couch, playing phone games, and binge-watching Netflix. Help them discover what invigorates them so they will have a life-long recreation to turn to when they face the stresses of life.

Reading for Fun

I read every day for my job. Pastor Larry Alberts of Way of the Lord church in Blaine, Minnesota, told me early on in my ministry, "Leaders are readers." I always have books on my coffee table at home and my desk at work that I am trying to work my way through. Notice, I used the word 'work' in the previous sentence. Although these books are beneficial, I would not call them 'fun.' I like to read well-written fiction to relax. Presently, my goal is to read four Pulitzer Prize novels this year. I find if I keep them on the table next to my chair in the living room, I will read instead of veg out on a TV program.

Reading for fun doesn't have to be an expensive hobby. Most churches have a small library that is filled with good Christian fiction. If that's not your thing, there is always the public library. I've found I enjoy reading e-books, and one of the best investments I've made to promote this is a tablet. You can download hundreds of books on your platform of choice and have them readily accessible wherever you go. I take my tablet with me when I travel, which saves me from having to drag around physical books, considering I tend to switch between reading for fun and reading for work.

> The public library is a great way to access books for free.

My wife loves to read too, and she joined our church's reading group to encourage this habit. Each month, the group reads one book and then meets to discuss it. There are reading groups in almost any city in the country, and these groups can also be an excellent way to meet new people and share ideas. Meetup.com is an online website that promotes groups. Just type in 'book club' and see what comes up in your area.

Physical Exercise

For many people, the words 'fun' and 'physical exercise' are never found in the same sentence. For others, they can't enjoy themselves unless they're sweating profusely. 1 Thessalonians 5:23 says, "Now may the God of peace himself sanctify you completely, and may your whole spirit and soul and body be kept blameless at the coming of our Lord Jesus Christ."

David Stine writes about the importance of a balanced life in his book, *The Whole Life*. As a pastor of one of the fastest-growing churches in the Washington D.C. area, he found he was unbalanced in his approach to ministry. David spent countless hours reading his Bible, praying, and fasting; however, he was neglecting his physical needs, and at the height of his success as a church builder, he became very sick. Now, he promotes a balance between spirit, soul, and body. He says, "It's amazing how focusing on all three areas instead of just one brought about unprecedented health and fulfillment in my life."[xii]

I have had my share of ups and downs in the area of physical fitness. I've probably lost and gained back over a thousand pounds in my life. That's why they call it the battle of the bulge. You have to fight to stay fit. One thing for sure is I'm able to have more fun when I'm in decent shape than when I'm not. When I was in prison, it was easy to stay fit. I had a lot of time to kill, so I would lift weights twice a day. This training also helped me release pent up energy and emotion. On the outside,

I have to work to make time for exercise, especially as a pastor and family man with four children.

You will need to do the same. Try not to let life's demands consume so much of you that you don't make time for yourself. You will be more productive if you set aside a few hours a week for fun and self-care. As you get older, you will find the quote by Hall of Famer Mickey Mantle to be applicable: "If I had known how long I was going to live, I'd have taken better care of myself."

Tips for Family and Friends

Tip #1 – Plan fun activities with your newly released loved one.

My mom's two brothers, Rick and Ron, are avid golfers. Playing with them has helped me see them in a different light. They have allowed me to enter their inner circle as one of the guys. Inviting a loved one to join you in your chosen recreational activities will show him/her you do not take yourself too seriously. Plus, it will show your fun side. It may even help them relive a bit of their childhood, which will bring healing to their wounded souls.

Competition has a way of revealing people's inner character. My Uncle Rick said, "If you want to know what a man is like in business, take him golfing." As a life-long salesman, he could tell if the man he was working with had integrity or not based on their conduct on the golf course. He told me, "Golf is a gentleman's sport, and each man must penalize himself for errant shots. If he cheats on the course, he will likely cheat you in business." You may get a glimpse into how well the released prisoner is doing based on their conduct during your playtime. For example, if it seems like they lack patience during a friendly game of basketball, you then have an opportunity to pray for the Lord to help them in this area.

Tip #2 – Participate in an activity that is of their choosing.

I'm not a big video game guy. When I was a kid, we had the first-generation Atari system that included games like Pong and Pac Man. In a family of eight kids, there was a lot of jostling as to whose turn it was. I got tired of it pretty quickly, so I returned to the privacy of my own bedroom to read and left the digital battling to my siblings.

My kids recently began convincing me to join their clan in a phone game called Clash of Clans. At first, I was resistant to the idea; however, they were having so much fun with it that I finally caved to the pressure. I joined under the codename Daddy Walrus, and my children have had a wonderful time teaching the old man how to set up my township and win battles. There are many important things I could do with my time instead of playing Clash of Clans, but this online game has helped me bond with them on their turf.

Try to find out what your loved one's passions are and show some interest. Perhaps they might invite you into their inner circle. It may end up being a basis for more in-depth conversations and relationships.

Questions for Discussion

1. Did you play sports or have some kind of extra-curricular activities when you were in high school? Share some memories of your experiences.

2. Did your parents force their idea of fun on you? How did that make you feel about that kind of recreation?

3. Why do you think work tends to consume our lives?

4. What are some of the activities you have enjoyed on the inside? What makes them fun for you?

5. How do you plan to have fun on the outside?

6. If you had to give yourself a rating between 1-10 in the areas of spirit, soul, and body, how do you think you're doing? Is your life balanced?

7. What are your thoughts on the importance of physical exercise? How do you plan on staying in shape when you get out?

Part IV
Leaving a Legacy

Become a Pillar in Society

"Let the thief no longer steal, but rather let him labor, doing honest work with his own hands, so that he may have something to share with anyone in need."
Ephesians 4:28

"Won't you be my neighbor?"
Mr. Rogers

The definition of a pariah is an individual that society rejects as an outcast. Many people on the outside do not want to deal with pariahs because they are the dregs of humanity. This is why we build prisons. Everyday citizens want criminals removed as far from society as possible. Consider England's solution to the problem of crime in the 16th and 17th centuries. Between 1788 and 1868, about 162,000 convicts were transported from Britain and Ireland to various penal colonies in Australia. Prisons in Great Britain were so overcrowded that officials began housing convicts in hulks (ships that were no longer seaworthy). When these reached their capacity, they needed a more permanent solution. Initially, they sent felons to America, but then the Revolution started and they turned to The Land Down Under. The very first settlement in Australia was Botany Bay, a penal colony that housed 11 ships filled with prisoners.[xiii]

Many of those convicts chose to stay put once they were released instead of returning to England. Some even became prominent figures in Australian society, and today, having a former prisoner in your family lineage, is seen as a cause for celebration. About 20% of the country's citizens can trace their heritage back to a transported convict. These initially cast-out ex-offenders had transitioned from being pariahs to pillars in their communities.[xiv]

I was a pariah, a parasite that sucked the lifeblood out of my family and workplace. I was a taker, only focused on my selfish desires. As prisoners, you are the pariahs of creation, cast out of the mainstream to this place where hired sentries keep you under control and separated from citizens.

Rather, should I say, you *were* a pariah! You were the reason for countless nightmares. You were a sex addict prowling for your next conquest. You were the cause for a million tears on a million cheeks. That has all changed because of the transformative power of the Holy Spirit. You have traversed the spiritual galaxy from darkness to light. According to Revelation 3:12, God sees you as pillars in his house. "He who overcomes, I will make him a pillar in the temple of my God, and he will go out from there no more. I will write on him the name of my God, and the name of the city of my God, the new Jerusalem, which comes down out of heaven from my God, and my own new name." The Apostle, John, declares this promise to the overcomer. That is what you are! You have conquered Satan and his evil schemes and plans for your life through the application of Romans 12:21, which tells us, "Do not be overcome by evil, but overcome evil with good."

'Good' is probably not a word that was used very often to describe your past life before Jesus poured out his precious blood upon you washing you clean, before God made you a pillar. Notice two realities about being God's pillar John touches upon. First, you are a pillar in his house, or as the passage calls it, his temple, the New Jerusalem. You will never be cast out again but will remain there forever. I find it curious that he compares us to pillars instead of floor tiles (or windows, stair railings, etc.). Pillars give support and strength to a house. Second, pillars often go unnoticed, blending into the background or hidden inside a wall. Try to take one away, though, and see how much you miss its absence.

The New Jerusalem is the capital city of the New Earth. It is the eternal city with streets of gold. God prepared it for those who have placed their trust in Christ. It's your future home! Furthermore, there are three names you wear as a pillar: God's name, the name of his city, and the secret name of Jesus. No more do you wear the shameful title of the State Corrections Department declaring to everyone you are one of the pariahs.

You are a pillar now!

Being established as pillars in God's house might seem like a lovely future event that will take place after Jesus returns, but the Scriptures make it clear that this is not some distant pie in the sky when you die occurrence. Ephesians 2:6 says God, "…raised us up with him [Jesus] and seated us with him in the heavenly places in Christ Jesus." Therefore, you are currently seated with Christ in heaven. We are giving strength and stability to God's house this very moment.

If you haven't already, begin to see yourself like that. You are powerful. You are essential to God's plan, no longer a taker, but rather a giver. As you reenter society, step into the call God has already ordained for you. Go forth, not as the scourge of society, but as the supporting structures, pillars in the house of our God.

A Military Example

At Fort Snelling in Minneapolis, there is a place called MEPS, which stands for Military Entrance Processing Station. All of the men and women who enter any of the five main branches of the military (Army, Navy, Air Force, Marines, and Coast Guard) are medically screened, academically evaluated, and finally sworn in at this building. I went through this whole process shortly before graduating from high school 33 years ago.

After I was sworn in that day, I was officially "in the Army." I jumped back on a Greyhound bus and returned to my home in Thorp, Wisconsin, to finish out my senior year. Even though I didn't look any different, dress any different, or even feel any different, I was considered military property. I had never fired a weapon, hadn't received any training, and in fact, I didn't even have a rank yet. But I had sworn an oath and had taken my stand. I was ready to stand up in defense of my country as a soldier in the United States Army.

Being saved is much like this. We have received Christ into our lives. He has done His saving work, and now we believe in him as our savior. But we don't look any different. We go back to our monotonous lives without any training in the Lord, carrying many of our same bad habits and mannerisms with us. But we are signed up! We are sworn in. We are in the Army of the Lord.

GET OUT FOR GOOD

What happens now? What are our marching orders? How do we go from being a plague upon society to contributing to the cure? In the U.S. military, it was easy. We received a letter containing our orders telling us when to arrive for the flight that would get us to basic training. After we finished there, we were sent off to our permanent duty station, where commanders told us where to sleep and eat, along with assigning daily tasks. But in Christianity, it isn't quite as clear. Each Christian becomes a pillar in their communities in thousands of different ways. One thing that remains the same is the foundation.

In the Army, where I was a soldier on the books, I still needed to have my body whipped into shape by drill sergeants in basic training, and then after that, commanding officers during my active duty. The purpose of this training was to turn me into a battle-ready soldier that, if war broke out, was prepared to fight. If we are to become pillars in our communities, engaging the enemy for the sake of others, we needed preparation.

> I still needed to have my body whipped into shape by drill sergeants.

It would have been extremely odd if I had jumped off the bus at Fort McClellan, Alabama, for boot camp and discovered my drill sergeants were recruits who had arrived the day before I did. We needed trained instructors that had seen battle up-close. My primary drill sergeant was a Vietnam veteran that had been on the front lines of combat. He knew the dangers we faced. He changed me from being a farm kid from Wisconsin into a warrior for the U.S. Army. Notice the process; I instantly *became* a soldier from the moment I signed up, but I was also *becoming* a soldier through the training I received.

You *are* a pillar in God's house, and you *are becoming* a pillar in your community through the influence of mature believers. There are Christian "drill sergeants" all around us. Unfortunately, they don't wear uniforms and insignia to help us recognize them, but they are out there nonetheless. To prepare for battle, you may have to seek them out. I've had many such instructors, each one focusing on distinct inadequacies that hindered my mission. They've addressed a variety of my shortcomings, such as selfishness, laziness, addictions, pleasure-seeking, and pride, to name a few of the hundreds of areas I needed training. That instruction continues to this day. I have not arrived. If you want to be a General in the United States Army, you are required to continue training throughout your career.

An Example from Seeds

Regarding my spirit and my life in Christ, God sees me as perfect. I am seated in the heavenly realm, where only perfectly holy things are allowed. Whenever the devil tries to discourage me and steal away my joy and assurance of salvation, I can look to the promise of Scripture that God has raised me up and made me spiritually alive in Jesus. The main problem is that we don't physically see this reality, only our weaknesses and failures. We see vain attempts to do the will of God, where we end up falling short of our ideals. As we consider the results of our efforts, they may not seem very noteworthy.

I saw an episode of a show on the History Channel that depicted life on earth after a natural disaster wiped out human beings. All the buildings began to topple after many years of decay, and on the show, they used computer generation to animate how this would happen. Massive cathedrals crashed down after hundreds of years of moisture and rot took a toll on these monuments. This temporality is the problem with earthly bodies. They are only a shadow of the things to come.

As 1 Corinthians 15:35, 37 says, "But someone will ask, 'How are the dead raised? With what kind of body do they come?' What you sow is not the body that is to be, but a bare kernel, perhaps of wheat or of some other grain." If I placed a kernel of grain in your hand, it would not look awe-inspiring. You might even mistake it for a piece of lint or a bit of debris that should be cast aside without another thought. If you put that seed in the ground though, and wait a few months, you'd have a new appreciation for its significance. Our lives here might not look like much; the daily choices we make for good may not seem to make much of an impact, but in the light of eternity, they produce an abundant harvest.

According to the USDA Economic Research Division, an acre of land has the potential of producing an average of about 33 bushels of wheat, enough to overflow your refrigerator and freezer twice. It only takes one bushel to plant that acre.[xv] That's a pretty substantial increase. As your life is sown into the community around you upon your release, you can anticipate an abundant harvest in eternity. Only in heaven will you see the full impact you made on the lives of others. Consider the difference between an acorn and a mighty oak tree. Jesus put it this way: "The kingdom of heaven is like a grain of mustard seed that a man took and sowed in his field. It is the smallest of all seeds, but when it has grown, it is larger than all the garden plants and becomes a tree so that the birds of the air come and make nests in its branches" (Matthew 13:31–32). As part of God's kingdom on earth, don't despise small beginnings.

Be an Overcomer

In the Revelation passage that speaks of how God makes us pillars in his house, there is a qualifier that says, "He who overcomes..." To make an impact on society, we need to overcome the kingdom of the devil. How do we do this? In our battle against Satan, we recognize that we are in the world, but not of it. We are Christ's ambassadors in enemy territory. In Matthew 28:18, Jesus told his followers, "All authority on earth and in heaven has been given into my hands, so go as my ambassadors and spread the Good News of the kingdom."

President Abraham Lincoln presented the Emancipation Proclamation to his Cabinet on July 22, 1862. In it he wrote, "...all persons held as slaves within any State... shall be then, thenceforward, and forever free; and the Executive Government of the United States, including the military and naval authority thereof, will recognize and maintain the freedom of such persons." Just because Lincoln declared this proclamation didn't mean every slave in America suddenly burst forth from their chains. It took a civil war to accomplish it. It wasn't until 1865 that the full realization of those words came to pass.

So, too, Jesus has made His emancipation proclamation in John 8:34, 36: "Truly, truly, I say to you, everyone who practices sin is a slave to sin. The slave does not remain in the house forever; the son remains forever. So, if the son sets you free, you will be free indeed." This offer for freedom in the son is all-inclusive because, in John 3:16, Jesus said, "For God so loved the world that he sent His only son..." Most of our friends and neighbors are still stuck in the chains of slavery to sin. They think just because they haven't gone to prison like you, they are not in captivity.

The Federal Writers Project reports that many U.S. slaves didn't know they were free for over a year after the Civil War ended. It wasn't until government officials came around and began to ask them questions about how they were compensated for their work that they learned the good news.[xvi] As ambassadors of Christ, we are those messengers! The devil is the slave master and doesn't want people to know they can be free! Thus, it is our job to let them know.

Revelation 12:11 reveals the secret to overcoming the devil's evil plan. "And they have conquered him [the devil] by the blood of the Lamb and by the word of their testimony, for they loved not their lives even unto death." When you walk over to your unbelieving neighbor's fence and begin to talk to them while they are weeding their garden, you are venturing into enemy territory. Your good looks, charisma, and ability to communicate smoothly will not free them from Satan's camp. Only the blood of Christ can do that, and the word of your testimony is the primary weapon you use. I have found arguing with someone about the Bible is not very fruitful. Instead, when I tell them how Jesus set me free, they are touched by the power of God's love. Don't be ashamed of your prison record. God is going to use it to set captives free.

Get Involved in Your Community

Pastor Kevin Harney of Shoreline Church in Monterey, California, has written a series of books on what he calls organic outreach. In his first book on the subject, *Organic Outreach for Ordinary People*, he states, "We want to share our faith but don't want to feel awkward, uncomfortable, or unnatural…for them or us!"[xvii] The bulk of the book describes how we can impact those around us through everyday activities such as sporting events, community groups, and service projects. He shows how we can take seemingly random events and turn them into opportunities to recapture those enslaved to sin and the devil.

I love this approach! Our church spent two years working to incorporate these practices into the fabric of every ministry. This method takes Holy Spirit awareness. It also requires going out into the community to the unbelievers. If we think we are going to sit in our pew at church and the heathens are going to come to us, we are sadly mistaken. It was easy for me to interact with non-Christians in prison; my situation forced me to live and work with them every day. Out in the real world, it's completely different. We live in a culture of reclusive people. Social media has caused us to isolate and shun direct contact with others. We would rather post something on Facebook than talk to a live person.

> Due to social media, we live in a culture of reclusive people.

You will need to find ways to connect with live human beings. This process may be through your job, a personal hobby, or a community project. As a barber, it was simple, as people came into my shop for 20 minutes a month, they expected me to talk with them while I was cutting their hair. Many times, those conversations turned into a discussion about the Lord. I tried not to force religious dialogue, but let it happen naturally. If they were going through something traumatic, I would listen and give them some biblical principles I'd found to be helpful in my life.

One customer I developed a relationship with using this approach was a man named Lennie. When he first strolled into my shop, he reminded me of a bulldog. He was short, muscular, and had a big personality. To make matters more interesting, he was an ex-pro wrestler working as a bail bondsman, and was 100% Italian. Whenever I talked with Lennie, I felt like I was in a scene from *The Godfather* and he was a hitman for the mob. For a decade, our friendship developed as he shared openly with me about family issues he dealt with, work-related stress he faced, and his Catholic upbringing.

On one afternoon in the week before Christmas, I was at home and received a call on my cell phone from Lennie, which was unusual. Immediately, I could tell from the tone of his voice something was wrong. He said he had been to the doctor and they told him he had stage-four esophageal cancer. I didn't know it at the time, but that's one of the worst types of cancer out there. I drove to his house and sat with him and his wife. I listened as they talked about their fears, especially in connection with their two grandchildren, who they were caring for in their home. I shared a simple Gospel message with Lennie, prayed for him, and cried with him. He gave me a big hug before I walked out the front door.

I spoke with Lennie a few times over the next couple of months, but he didn't want me to come over to his house. His wife told me privately he was too proud to let anyone see him in his weakened condition. Lennie was finally ready for me to visit the house in mid-February. His wife met me at the front door and walked me back to the bedroom. When I entered, I thought for a moment I was in the wrong room. Lennie had gone from a hulking, muscle-bound 260-pound force, to a 170-pound shell in less than two months. He reached out and took my hand, squeezing it weakly. In his North Minneapolis Italian accent, he said, "This was a tough one. The chemo beat me down. I don't think I have the strength to beat this, Scott." I reminded him again about one man who had conquered death. Lennie nodded in agreement and said, "Yes, I believe in him!" He died later that night. I was in seminary at the time, so I officiated his funeral the following week. To this day, I call Lennie's wife every year on the anniversary of his death.

Our task is to seek out the thousands of Lennies that are out there. As overcomers, go forth and set them free.

Tips for Family and Friends

Tip #1 – Focus more on your loved one's identity in Christ as opposed to their status as a felon.

Negative words can be very damaging to emotionally fragile people. Reentering society after a long absence might cause your loved one to feel very vulnerable. As parents and friends, we can easily fall into the trap of negative messages. We can unintentionally throw a wet blanket over their dreams with comments like, "That's a little beyond your ability to accomplish, don't you think?" or "Let's keep your expectations realistic." Those leaving prison will have numerous doubts about their ability to succeed as a pillar in society. We can speak life to them by trying to catch a vision from the Lord about how he sees them.

164172. That was the number I received from the Minnesota Corrections Department so they could track me effortlessly through the system. I don't think I will ever forget it. My identity in Christ is not tied to that number and what it represents. Ephesians 1:3-4 says, "Blessed be the God and Father of our Lord Jesus Christ, who has blessed us in Christ with every spiritual blessing in the heavenly places, even as he chose us in him before the foundation of the world, that we should be holy and blameless before him." According to this passage, I am blessed, chosen, and blameless. Help your loved one see their destiny is not as a pariah to society; they can become a pillar because of the power of the Holy Spirit working mightily in them.

Tip #2 – Be honest about the effects of the ex-offender's crimes.

This tip may seem to contradict the previous one, but know there will be times you might need to talk with your loved one about how the decisions of their past impacted you. One of the least helpful things someone can say to a person who is trying to apologize to them is, "It's fine. Don't worry about it." Steps eight and nine of the Alcoholics Anonymous program state:

- Made a list of all persons we had harmed and became willing to make amends to them all.
- Made direct amends to such people wherever possible, except when to do so would injure them or others.

Part of the process of becoming a pillar in society is taking responsibility for our past actions. Confession, forgiveness, and reconciliation are crucial rungs on the ladder that help ex-cons climb out of the hole of self-loathing.

Questions for Discussion

1. Why do you think the attitude toward having a criminal in your family line has changed over time in Australia?

2. The majority of society views prisoners as pariahs. How does this make you feel about yourself?

3. Think about all the bad things you have done in your life. In contrast, what does doing good look like for you? For example, Scott stole from many people, but now desires to do good by giving back to his community.

4. Why is it so hard to remember that, from God's perspective, we are seated with Christ in the heavenly realm?

5. Ephesians 6 talks about how our struggle (battle) is not against flesh and blood; it's against the spiritual forces of darkness. Using modern military terminology, describe ways the Christian engages in that battle. For example, prayer is like a walkie-talkie that has a direct line to the General (God).

6. What are some of the natural ways you plan to interact with unbelievers when you get out?

7. Think about Scott's relationship with Lennie. What do you think caused Lennie to trust Scott enough to invite him to his death bed?

When You Fall, Get Back Up

"For the righteous falls seven times and rises again."
Proverbs 24:16

"To those who love God, sin is suffering; it is not voluntary doing. But even this can be turned into purpose by our Lord."
C.O. Rosenius

Joshua was God's chosen man to lead the people of Israel into the Promised Land. In Joshua 13, he is about to retire as commander of the armies of Israel after fighting battles over five decades. But if you look at the map of the areas he conquered, they fall short of the amount of land God initially promised Abraham. At the end of Joshua's life, we see there are still many unconquered lands that need to be eradicated in the future. The area promised to Abraham includes all of modern-day Jordan, half of Iraq, half of Syria, a quarter of Saudi Arabia, and a quarter of Egypt. In other words, it was a much larger area than they had settled. This is why God makes this statement to

Joshua in verse 13:1; "You are old and advanced in years, and there remains yet very much land to possess."

Why didn't the Lord just have them conquer the entire Promised Land all at once? As Christians, we may wonder the same thing about the 'unconquered lands' in our own lives. You see, each of us has our own 'season of Joshua.' It's that time when we are first released from the bondage of sin, like the Israelites were set free from Egypt. We enter into the Promised Land of salvation and life in Christ. The victories seem to come easily. God flattens Jericho right in front of us without us having to lift a finger. The truth is we needed God to eradicate a good portion of these sinful habits in order to experience some stability without losing heart and running back to Egypt.

Israel experienced great success in battle under the leadership of Joshua, and this struck fear into the hearts of the nations around them. This achievement allowed them to begin to settle in and live productive lives in the Promised Land.

At some point, that season came to an end, as it does for us, and we are confronted with many unconquered lands. We face deeply entrenched and stubborn sins that are in opposition to the promised life God wants for us. There are a few reasons he allows this.

When You Stumble, You Get Humble

First, those areas of struggle keep us humble. One of the characteristics new Christians seem to share is the perception that overcoming sin is simple, and they look down on struggling believers. When I was a new Christian in prison, I had a long list of rules I thought real Christians should follow, as opposed to the slackers. Real Christians didn't drink, smoke, or watch R-rated movies; they attended church every Sunday, only listened to Christian radio, and turned every conversation into a witnessing opportunity. In my arrogance I unfairly judged anyone who didn't have the same high standard of Christian living I did.

Within a short period after my conversion, I began to face some of my unconquered lands. As you may have guessed, spiritual pride was the first enemy to threaten the border of my perfect Promised Land-life. As the Lord began to expose some of those weaknesses, it humbled me. It was a warning to not scorn others who seemingly were not as far along in their Christian walk as me, although, in reality, they may have surpassed me in the sanctification process.

> Spiritual pride was the first enemy to threaten the border of my Promised Land.

If the people of Israel had conquered all the land that was promised to Abraham back in Genesis, they would have been the leading superpower of the day. To go from Egyptian slave to ruler of the most powerful country on the planet in less than 100 years would have been too much for their egos. These lands were left for future generations to defeat in order for Israel to mature until it could handle the power.

We have seen the self-destructive results that power and land-hungry leadership can have in people like Alexander the Great. From the time he succeeded his father, at age 20, as the Greek king of Macedon until his untimely death at the age of 32, he led one of the most successful military campaigns in the history of humanity. He was never defeated in battle and conquered much of Northern India and Africa, along with most of the civilized world. One account of his death says he drank a bowl of unmixed wine in honor of Hercules and was dead within two weeks.

Hitler's hunger for land and conquest is notorious. In fact, most believe he would have won WWII if he had not cast his power-lusting gaze on Russia. A divided front finally did him in and at the age of 56 he committed suicide in an underground bunker as the Allied troops took Berlin.

God's ultimate goal for Joshua was not to become the leader of the largest country in the world. It was for him to lead God's people into a land of peace and freedom, not the madness and strife that come from leaders like Hitler or Alexander the Great. So too, for us, God's desire is not to turn us into powerhouse mega-Christians, but to recapture our hearts as His sons and daughters.

Excessive Righteousness?

Secondly, if Joshua had taken all the land, the people would have become worn out. Doing everything perfectly in life will wear you out quickly! I haven't met too many perfectionists that are fun to be around. Just ask my kids what their dad is like when he is in his perfectionist mode. God knew precisely what the people of Israel could handle.

I think we here in America have a difficult time realizing what life in modern-day Israel must be like. At its widest point, it is only 85 miles across. They are surrounded by hostile countries, which is why compulsory military conscription is in place. Every man has to serve three years in the military and every woman serves two years. In times of war, every able-bodied citizen can be called upon to fight.

Ancient Israel faced a similar plight. They were on constant alert, and it took all their diligence and resources to keep the land they had captured secure. Imagine if their borders were ten times as long! They would have been completely exhausted trying to defend them. Living a righteous life can be somewhat exhaust-

GET OUT FOR GOOD 179

ing for the modern-day Christian. This difficulty is why Gal 6:9 encourages us: "Let us not become weary in doing good, for at the proper time we will reap a harvest if we do not give up." There are so many worldly distractions, and at certain times God wants us to focus on one particular border in our lives that needs full defense.

There is a strange passage in Ecclesiastes 7:16 where Solomon warns his sons, "Do not be excessively righteous and do not be overly wise. Why should you ruin yourself?" When I first read this a long time ago, it shocked me. Isn't my goal as a Christian to be righteous in every area of my life? Now let me preface this next statement by saying God does want us to have victory in every area of our lives over the world, the flesh, and the devil. Nevertheless, I am convinced that cannot be fully achieved in this life. Instead, we fight the battle God places in front of us for the moment and we leave that unconquered land for another time. We don't fight 1,000 different campaigns on as many fronts continually. If we do, we will ruin ourselves and become like the legalistic Pharisees who thought favor with God was achieved by following hundreds of rules.

God's Workmanship

Finally, we recognize the constant need for God to finish the work. One of the passages in Scripture that has brought me great comfort in my struggle with sin is Romans 7:15. Paul the Apostle provides an inside look at his own battles with the flesh. "I do not understand what I do. For what I want to do, I do not do, but what I hate I do." Have you ever experienced this in your life? Were you determined to incorporate Christian disciplines into your life like daily devotions, fasting, praying, and witnessing to others, but you came up short of your lofty goals?

The Importance of the Gospel

Many times, the reason we fail is we are not fighting the battle in the right way. Notice in Joshua 13:6, the Lord tells of His plans for Israel. "I myself will drive them out from before the people of Israel." When we fight multiple battles with our own will, we find ourselves exclaiming with Paul, "I don't do what I want to and do the things I despise." But Paul had discovered the key in the struggle, as evident in verse 24-25 of Romans 7: "Wretched man that I am! Who will deliver me from this body of death? Thanks be to God through Jesus Christ, our Lord!"

In Scripture, the original languages defined sin as "missing the mark." The mark, of course, is the perfect will of God in any given situation. A few months ago, I actually set out to not sin for as long as I could. A problem soon arose, because most of my focus had been on not doing certain things (don't covet, don't grumble, don't waste time at work, etc.). Then I began to take into consideration what are called sins of omission. James 4:17 says, "Anyone, then, who knows the good he ought to do and doesn't do it, sins." Not to mention the greatest commandment set forth by Jesus, to love the Lord my God with all my heart, soul, and strength. And then there's the "loving your neighbor as yourself" problem.

By the next morning, I was feeling pretty depressed. I found great encouragement in 1 John 2:1. "My little children, I am writing these things to you so that you may not sin. But if anyone does sin, we have an advocate with the Father, Jesus Christ the righteous." John knows Christians are still going to miss the mark. He knows these defeats will cause them to become discouraged and want to quit the war. That is why he reminds us of the sweet Gospel message.

He is Our Advocate

The sense of the word 'advocate' is one who pleads another's cause or stands in their defense. Essentially, Jesus is our heavenly lawyer in the courtroom of God. The question is who is the prosecutor? Some think God is the prosecutor, but take notice of Romans 8:33: "Who shall bring any charge against God's elect? It is God who justifies." No, it's the devil that is called the accuser of the brethren.

But he's not the only one that is continually trying to condemn us. It is stated in 1 John 3:20, "If our hearts condemn us, we know that God is greater than our hearts, and he knows everything." Your heart can be the most significant source of condemnation. These sources of unreliable condemnation are why we need Jesus, the advocate.

Another way advocate can be defined is 'one who comforts.' When you sin and then repent, you sometimes continue to beat yourself up. "I'm supposed to be a Christian, and I did that again!" This is when the comforting words of Jesus are so important. They will lift us from the pit of despair and encourage us not to give up the fight.

Jesus spoke to Peter in Luke 5:8-9, and I have found those words to be extremely comforting. The Lord had just performed the miracle of the miraculous catch of fish. Peter realizes who he is and falls at his

> Depart from me, Lord, for I am a sinful man!

feet; "Depart from me, Lord, I am a sinful man!" But Jesus lifts

Peter's face and looks in His eyes and says, "Do not be afraid." Many times, when we realize we have sinned, we do the opposite of what we should. We run from God and hide in the bushes like Adam and Eve did when they ate from the tree of the knowledge of good and evil. What we should do is run to him! I remember different times when my kids would come to me and confess something they had done. Man, they sure looked relieved that they had gotten that off their chests and restored our relationship.

He is Our Propitiation

The Apostle continues in 1 John 2:2; "He is the propitiation for our sins, and not for ours only but also for the sins of the whole world." Propitiation is the means by which God's character becomes consistent with His actions. For instance, say my 15-year-old son, Seth, gets invited to go to Six Flags with his youth group, but then he remembers he is scheduled to work that day. He comes to me and asks, "Dad, can't I just call my boss and tell him about Six Flags?" Being the awesome father I am, I say, "No, son. You have a responsibility to your job first." While we are having this conversation, it just so happens that Seth's friend is standing nearby and overhears us. He steps up and says, "Pastor Stroud, I can work for Seth so he can go to Six Flags."

As a loving father, I wanted Seth to be able to go to Six Flags, but his responsibility for work stood in the way. Seth's friend became the propitiation that allowed both criteria to be met; his boss would have a worker, and Seth would have his fun day. God's nature is loving and merciful, but he is also just. Jesus became the means by which he could be both just and merciful.

During his time at Six Flags, I would venture to say that Seth would probably be thinking about his friend quite a bit. Remembering what Jesus did for us will help us, not only when we sin, but also when we are *about* to sin. We may pause and question, "How can I trample on the grace of God by continuing in things that displease him?"

For the Whole World

I want to draw your attention to this powerful phrase that John uses when he speaks of the propitiation Christ offers. The offer of forgiveness of sins is not for just a pre-selected group of people. God so loved the entire world, and whoever believes in him will not perish but will have eternal life. With this knowledge, we can confidently go out and proclaim the good news to whomever is out there.

There are many that struggle under the enormous burden of sin that need to hear this liberating message. Perhaps today, it's you. Have you ever been to a shooting range for target practice? Obviously, the point is to try to hit the bullseye. Your chances of doing that increase significantly if you incorporate certain things into your shooting routine. First of all, a gun is helpful. If I have a target that is 300 yards downrange, using my own strength to throw a bullet that far would be pretty fruitless. Many people try to live moral lives without the power of God working within them. It's called "attempting to be good." But Jesus made it clear there is only one who is good—God. If you want to overcome sin, you need the proper weapon to battle it, namely the sword of the spirit, which is the Word of God.

The second thing that might be helpful in hitting the target would be a scope. This handy apparatus will help to bring the target into focus much more clearly than your natural vision.

God gives every Christian a "scope" known as the Holy Spirit. His job is to convict us when we sin, to comfort us when we are in despair, and to lead us as we make daily decisions. But maybe you find yourself getting tired of always trying to hit the bullseye day after day. You want to throw the scope to the side, grab a 50-caliber machine gun and just point downrange and let 'er fly. That may be fun for the moment, but brace yourself for a lot of unintended damage.

Finally, if you want to hit the target, getting down in the prone position and bracing yourself against an embankment is much more useful than just standing tall and trying to do so. Our embankment is the church. As the Body of Christ, we steady and support one another as we try to hit the target of God's intended holiness.

When a person goes to the range, they rarely put every bullet right in the center of the target, but at least they are practicing to do so. This is the Christian life. You may not hit the bullseye every time, but don't give up trying. When you fall, don't just lay there, letting the devil kick you while you're down. Struggle to your feet and get back in the war!

Tips for Family and Friends

Tip #1 – Your Loved One will Stumble in Their Reentry Process.

We hope those getting out of prison, rehab, and transitional housing will never fall. The reality is they will because, as Jesus' brother says in James 3:2, "We all stumble in many ways." Our biggest concern should be what they do once they fall. Ex-offenders are idealistic about life on the outside; they think it's going to be easier once they hit the streets. They believe they will be so busy living life they will not have time to make the same mistakes they made that caused them to offend in the first place.

As a member of their support system, focus more on the deeper issues than you do their missteps. Be willing to have meaningful conversations with them about their past and the emotional turmoil they are feeling. When they are depressed because they have stumbled, help them get back in the game like a good coach who assists his players in seeing the big picture after a tough loss.

Tip #2 – Focus on the Gospel more than the Law.

Most prisoners have heard plenty about how bad they are from police officers, judges, correction officers, and the media. If they have had a legitimate conversion, they will feel terrible about their crimes and the pain they have caused others. What they need to hear the most from their friends and families are messages of hope. Faith believes in unseen things, and even though your loved one may not be currently walking in the complete freedom you hope for, God is not finished with them yet. Have faith and don't give up on them!

A while back, I did an interview for our church radio show, The Harvest Report. I hosted a woman that another pastor told me had a vibrant prayer life. After our radio conversation, I invited her into the sanctuary and asked if she would be willing to pray and see if the Lord gave her any insight into our church. She went up to the front near the baptismal font while I watched her from back near the exit. After about five minutes, she came back and told me she had a sense from the Lord. She said, "It's a message for you, Pastor Scott. The Lord says to you, 'This is my beloved son with whom I am well pleased.'" That was quite a shock to me because the previous week I had been struggling in my ministry. I had a besetting sin that seemed to be getting the best of me, and I felt very far from being pleasing to the Lord.

As I thought more about this message, it dawned on me. As a Christian, I am in Christ. When God looks at me, he sees his beloved son. It's not about how well I perform or overcome sins in my life that make me pleasing to the Lord. It is the blood of Jesus that covers me that makes me pleasing to him. Remind your son, daughter, or friend about this reality. Help them see who God has made them to be rather than who they think they are in a weak moment.

Questions for Discussion

1. Talk about some of the unconquered lands you are currently facing and the false messages the devil is trying to convince you of about yourself.

2. What are some of the areas you have already found success in by God's grace? How were you able to overcome those areas?

3. C. O. Rosenius said, "To those who love God, sin is suffering; it is not voluntary doing. But even this can be turned into purpose by our Lord." Explain how God can use our failings for his purposes.

4. Do you have a list of rules you impose upon others regarding the Christian life? How do you feel when you see others not living up to your standard?

5. Solomon said, "Do not be excessively righteous and do not be overly wise. Why should you ruin yourself?" How does excessiveness ruin people?

6. Explain your perception of the Gospel. Why is it so crucial for the ex-offender to have a Gospel-dominated life?

7. What is your game plan for when you stumble in the area of former addictions?

Give Back

"Always being prepared to make a defense to anyone who asks
you for a reason for the hope that is in you."
1 Peter 3:15

"Remember your chains."
Steven Curtis Chapman

During our family travels around the country, we spotted many signs along the way known as Historical Markers. These markers tell stories and point out facts about significant events and people from those locations. There are thousands of these markers throughout the U.S.

Erecting historical markers is not a new concept only found in America. In ancient times, there were markers erected from the simple to the grandiose. The Egyptians built the pyramids in Giza in 2500 BC, mainly as a historical marker of the life of Pharaoh Khufu. In contrast, one of the simplest historic markers rested next to the Jordan River not too far from Jericho. It was a humble pile of 12 stones taken from the middle of the river and piled up together as a memorial. Although this monument was not as elaborate as the millions of stones it took to build the pyramids, it was, nonetheless, very significant. We see the account in Joshua 4:3, "Take twelve stones from here out of the midst of the Jordan, from the very place where the priests' feet stood firmly, and bring them over with you and lay them down in the place where you lodge tonight."

These 12 stones represented the direct interaction of the living God in the lives of a seemingly insignificant slave-tribe. They were reminders of how God had taken them from the banks of the Nile River to the Jordan River. When the descendants of those present at its dedication later asked what these stones signified, there were four important events the people of Israel related. These events have direct correlations in your life as one who God set free, both physically and spiritually.

God Brought Them out of Bondage

In 1994, the contemporary Christian artist Steven Curtis Chapman wrote a song entitled "Remember Your Chains." He wrote it on an airplane when he saw a man being led on board in shackles by federal officers. It caused him to think about the chains he was bound in before Jesus saved him. Here is a portion of the lyrics.

> Remember your chains
> Remember the prison that once held you
> Before the love of God broke through
> Remember the place
> You were without grace
> When you see where you are now
> Remember your chains
> And remember your chains are gone

When God told the people of Israel to erect this memorial near the Jordan River, he was telling them, "Never forget what I have freed you from." Unfortunately, this is precisely what happened in the life of Israel after they entered the Promised Land. The following generations became comfortable and ambivalent in their walk with the Lord and even began to envy the nations around them. They didn't remember their chains. They didn't recall that God brought them out by His mighty wonders. They didn't continue to serve the Lord, but instead turned to idols.

As ex-offenders, we can forget our chains. When we are initially released from the bondage of sin and death, we are ecstatic! We have eternal life in Christ and are free from the bondage to sin that has held us captive for so many years. Later, when we are released from the corrections system, we may have grand plans regarding how we are going to serve the Lord by ministering to those who are still in bondage all around us.

But at some point, we can become lax in our zeal for the Lord. We may even begin to dabble again in the very sins that held us captive and caused us to offend in the first place. When you start to see that attitude creep into your life, then the words of Joshua become very relevant. "Take twelve stones… and lay them down in the place where you lodge tonight."

Perhaps your remembrance stone can be as simple as a picture that reminds you of the bondage of the former life you lived. I have pictures of myself from that period, where even the look on my face shows the chains were still binding me. I have photos of myself in prison that I regularly take out and look at, remembering how I felt while I was still incarcerated.

Another stone of remembrance you might have could be an actual stone. They sell small, polished stones at some Christian bookstores that have different words like grace, forgiveness, love, and so on inscribed on them. Purchasing one and carrying it around in your pocket can help you recall the bondage from which God has set you free.

Alcoholics Anonymous has captured this principle with tokens that state the number of days, months, or years that one has stayed sober. This small coin reminds them of all the days they chose not to drink. It reminds them of their decision to cry out to God for release.

Paul encouraged the believers in Galatia with these words: "For freedom Christ has set us free; stand firm therefore, and do not submit again to a yoke of slavery" (Galatians 5:1). Once we have trusted in Christ, we have the decision whether or not we will submit to the bondage of our sin again. Remember your chains! And remember your chains are gone!

God Revealed Their Sin

The next milestone this memorial was supposed to help them to remember might not seem like something you would want to remember with fondness. It is the fact that God revealed to the Israelites His Holy Law. They would not have known they were sinning against God and would have remained in ignorant bliss if they had not received His commands on Mount Sinai.

Paul talks about this very thing in Romans 7:7-9:

> "Yet if it had not been for the Law, I would not have known sin. For I would not have known what it is to covet if the Law had not said, 'You shall not covet.' But sin, seizing an opportunity through the commandment, produced in me all kinds of covetousness. For apart from the Law, sin lies dead. I was once alive apart from the Law, but when the commandment came, sin came alive, and I died."

Some might say then, why did God give the Law? Why didn't he just leave us in our ignorant state? The main reason is that ignorance of the Law does not excuse the lawbreaker. We are still in danger of punishment even if we are unaware of the Law. We see this in our local police departments. Many have received a ticket for something that they didn't know was wrong. Sometimes an officer will give you a warning for breaking a law you didn't know you were violating. I have been given warnings for a tail light I didn't realize was burned out, even though the officer could have given me a citation.

God was giving us a sign when he selected Israel from among the nations of the earth to reveal His Law to them. He was giving humanity a warning ticket. He explained to them that he was not happy with their deeds and punishment would be inevitable if things didn't change. It is like a CT scan at the doctor's office. Sure, you could go on ignoring the symptoms your body sends you and continue denying you have cancer or heart disease, but then you would not have a chance to catch it early and deal with it. God's revelation of the Law was a gift to the people of Israel, although I'm sure it didn't feel like much of a gift at the time. It was something for them to remember. As you remember your chains, thank the Lord he revealed the sinfulness of your life, and continues to do so day by day. He has offered you the chance to deal with your issues before it's too late.

God Led Them Through the Desert

One of the wonders about the journey of the Israelites into the Promised Land is how God did not abandon them the first time they refused to enter in. It's like he said, "Ok. It looks like we are going to need to purify this bunch a bit before they are ready for the blessings I have ahead for them." Remember that

God had commanded the ten spies be sent to scout out the land, and he knew what their report was going to be. But he did not forsake them but continued to watch over them for forty years in the wilderness, as those who had refused to enter died off until there were only two of the originals left.

The Israelites are a fantastic picture of our own life in this world. God could just zap us to heaven as soon as we accept Jesus as our Savior. However, he chooses to keep us here in the wilderness of this world. I believe the main reason is he wants us to be an example to those who are still in bondage to sin and the devil. The people of Israel were to be an example to the surrounding pagan nations.

When we look back in remembrance of these times of wandering around in the desert, we can do so with thankfulness because Romans 8:28 tells us that "all things work together for good to them that love the Lord and are called according to His purpose." He knows we need preparation so we can fulfill his purposes. It is good to remember those dry times in your life when God seemed so distant because you can encourage others as they go through dry times.

God Made a Way for Them into the Promised Land

In Joshua 7:14, we see God used this crossing of the Jordan as a way to exalt Joshua in the eyes of the people. Just as they had seen the parting of the Red Sea through Moses, they now saw Joshua part the Jordan. The name of Joshua is pronounced Yehōshu'a in the Hebrew and Aramaic. Just as Michael is many times shortened to Mike, Yehōshu'a was many times shortened to Yeshu'a. In English, we translate Yeshu'a into the name Jesus. We see a direct tie from Joshua to Jesus as one who led the people into the Promised Land.

It is evident in Scripture that God has parted the river of death. We can cross over because of the work that Christ did on the cross. John 3:36 states, "Whoever believes in the son has eternal life; whoever does not obey the son shall not see life, but the wrath of God remains on him." He is the only way to cross over the Jordan River of death into eternal life. We have not yet crossed over into the Promised Land of heaven, but many of our loved ones have. Wouldn't it be great if they could come back and give us a description? Scripture gives an account of some who have gone to the other side and reported back about heaven. John wrote the entire book of Revelation about it, Paul received a vison of the eternal, and Jesus was originally from there and spoke quite a bit about heaven.

> Jesus is the only way to cross the river of death into eternal life.

Some people avoid thinking about and reading about heaven. They say they don't want to bother with future glory since there is much to concentrate on now. I disagree with this attitude because the more we understand about eternity the more we will realize how short our time is here in the world. Thinking about heaven should motivate us to tell others about the Gospel message. Consider for a moment some of the amazing promises we see in the Bible regarding heaven:

- We will have no more pain.
- We will have all the tears wiped from our eyes.
- We will no longer mourn.
- We will live forever without getting old.
- We will rule and reign with Christ.
- We will see our saved relatives who have passed before us.
- We will have our own heavenly mansions to dwell in.

If you knew about a vacation destination on this earth that had even one of these listed benefits, wouldn't you tell everyone you knew about that place?

You Have Special Credibility

Think about all those men and women in prison who are still in bondage to sin. They are spiritually dead. I can think of no one better to tell them about freedom in Christ than one who has experienced the same things they are going through. As a released prisoner, you have a story to share that lends you significant credibility in prisons. This is not to say a Christian with no criminal past cannot effectively minister to convicts. The Word of God is powerful, and it will accomplish its purpose no matter who brings it through the prison gates. But it seems those in prison sit up and take special notice when one of their own comes to preach.

Toil with His Energy

I would add a warning for those who desire to begin to minister once they get out. There is a certain amount of preparation and maturity that is required to do so effectively. God also has a particular method he wants us to use. Paul's ministry was an example of this method. He writes about it in Colossians 1:28-2:3. Paul begins by saying in verse 28-29, "Him we proclaim, warning everyone, and teaching everyone with all wisdom, that we may present everyone mature in Christ. For this, I toil, struggling with all his energy that he powerfully works within me."

A typical conversation that takes place among our children is regarding superheroes. The main question is, "If you could have any superpower, what would it be?" Some typical responses include power of flight, invisibility, super strength, and bad breath that could kill your enemy. Paul tells us he toils with superhuman strength. He has superpowers! And he doesn't have to select just one power, as he has at his disposal the Holy Spirit's power to accomplish his task. Consider some of Jesus' superhuman powers:

- He walked on water.
- He could walk through an angry mob that wanted to kill him, unharmed.
- He had control over the weather.
- He could defeat demons and order them around.
- He could multiply food.
- He could fly.
- He could find treasure that a fish had swallowed.
- He knew the future.
- If you killed him, he would rise from the dead even more powerful than before!

These are the kinds of superpowers I would love to have. These are the powers Paul accessed! These powers gave him the ability to face incredible opposition, even to the point that people thought they had killed him, but he would show up the next day preaching the Gospel.

If we want to minister to the lost, we need to do so in the power that Christ supplies. We need to get in tune with what the Holy Spirit is doing around us. Frankly, if we try to minister in our power, we are setting ourselves up for disappointment, burn out, and a major assault from the enemy.

During Jesus' time on earth, he wove a common thread through every experience and conversation. He only did what his Father in heaven was telling him to do. The way he heard this was through constant communication with him. He was always listening for the Father's voice in everything he did.

But you might say, "Well, he was God's son. Of course, he is going to have supernatural powers and be able to hear the voice of the Father." But note Jesus' ministry did not begin until he was baptized and the Holy Spirit descended upon him. After Jesus departed from this world, it wasn't until Pentecost, when the Holy Spirit came upon the disciples, that they went out boldly to accomplish their mission. Before this event, they were hiding from the authorities. The same Holy Spirit desires to work powerfully in our lives today! He will lead and guide you as you minister to others.

Admonish and Teach

The second thing I want you to note about Paul's approach to ministry is he took time to admonish and teach those under his care. There is a famous saying attributed to Saint Francis of Assisi. "Preach the Gospel, and if necessary, use words." For many, avoidance of speaking has become their predominant method of sharing Jesus. They feel their life is going to point people to the Lord. The problem is, as D. A. Carson states, it would be like a news reporter trying to do their job without using words. The message we bring is called the GOOD NEWS!

The way we live our lives will give credibility to our words, but people need to hear the message through words. There are dozens of times I can recall people speaking powerful things into my life. The Bible tells us in Proverbs 18:21 that "Death and life are in the power of the tongue, and those who love it will eat its fruits." In other words, the one who loves life will eat fruit from the words people speak.

One of my primary mentors is someone I have never met. His name is Clive. Most of the world knows him as C.S. Lewis. Even though I have seen pictures of him, I probably would not recognize him if I saw him on the streets—but I would recognize his words! I have read most of his books, even one over a dozen times. His words give me life.

We need to try to speak into people's lives. Don't let that word of encouragement or reproof go unspoken. Be sure you take a balanced approach. Many of us lean too heavily to one side or the other of the equation. Some have an easy time encouraging but struggle to confront a difficult situation. Others are quick to call someone to the carpet on a transgression but rarely praise a son, daughter, or student.

> Don't let that word of encouragement or reproof go unspoken.

As we speak to those we minister to, there are two primary goals. The first goal is for them to get to know Christ. Paul said he wanted to know Jesus and the power of His rising. One of the ways to get to know him is by spending time with people who know him better than we do. For people that don't know my wife, Mary, I can give them a pretty good description of who she is and what she likes. Now, ultimately, they will need to meet her someday if they really want to know her personally. It's the same with God. He doesn't want us to just know about him. He wants us to know him personally.

The second goal our words can accomplish is in regards to discipleship. The Christian life has many challenges. Leading someone in a prayer of salvation, giving them a Bible, and then sending them on their way does the body a great disservice. Sheep need to be led so they will not end up on the side of a cliff with a busted leg, or worse, in the teeth of the wolves. When the shepherd sees his sheep wandering off, he calls out to them and they recognize his voice. There are times the head shepherd is going to speak to his sheep through you. When Jesus gave the Great Commission, he told the Apostles to make disciples, "…teaching them all that I have commanded you."

Brace for Opposition

The devil hates when we minister to the lost. He hates when we devote our lives to discipleship. He doesn't want fully grown, battle-tested opponents to fight. He likes easy, vulnerable targets.

Your old friends in the world may not like the fact that you are maturing in Christ. You were a lot more "fun" before you began to have an opinion about right and wrong. Some spiritual leaders may not want you ministering to their "flock." They don't want them studying the Bible and doing research. They want them to rely entirely on everything they say, swallowing it hook, line, and sinker.

As those who care for the lives of those God has given us a burden for, we must not be surprised when we face opposition to our cause. Paul faced severe opposition to the point of being physically violated. He faced danger on every side. Ask yourself if you are willing to do whatever it takes to carry the Good News to the world. During the fight, remember the battle belongs to the Lord. He is fighting for those souls as well.

Look Beyond the Immediate

One of the most interesting verses to me in the Bible is Proverbs 17:6. "Grandchildren are the crown of the aged, and the glory of children is their fathers." Note the crown for a man is not his children. Instead, it is seeing whether or not the time and effort he spent raising his kids will get passed on to the next generation.

Paul had a long vision. He was concerned about this Gospel message taking hold among the Gentiles and spreading like crazy. He was so dedicated, he became a mentor to those he had never even seen. The Church in Colossae was one such example. They had been impacted by Epaphras, who was one of Paul's sons in the Lord. In other words, the members of the congregation in Colossae were Paul's spiritual grandchildren.

The goal of ministry is to reproduce what has been produced in us. One of my mentors measured manhood by the number of people you could care for. When you get out, your main task will be caring for yourself. As you mature, you will begin to care for more people. Giving back shows we recognize how God has used many people to shape and form us, and in gratitude we pay it forward.

Tips for Family and Friends

Tip #1 – Don't be embarrassed about your loved one's less-than-stellar past.

There will be awkward situations because of your loved one's criminal past. Perhaps someone will ask you how your son or daughter are doing, not knowing he or she is in prison, or has just gotten out. Be truthful and upfront about the struggles you are facing. Also, express the hope you have because of the transformative work the Lord is doing in their life. You never know who you might encourage. I have had dozens of meaningful conversations with people about my past because I was willing to be vulnerable with them about the struggles I've faced.

As a minister, I find people are relieved when they find out I have not lived a perfect life. They realize that if God can forgive and use me, he can do the same for them or someone they love. You may even develop a relationship around your shared burdens. Obviously, we want to protect our children's privacy, so get their permission ahead of time, especially if it is someone they both know.

Tip #2 – If your friend or relative is allowed to go back into prison to minister, offer to go with them.

A few years ago, my Uncle Rick was going to be in town for a visit. He asked me what I had going on that week, and when I told him I was going to be preaching in prison the Sunday he was here, he shocked me by asking if he could go with me. Listen to his account in his own words.

> "A few years ago, I had the opportunity to visit a Sunday service at Soledad prison with my nephew, Pastor Scott Stroud. The experience of entering the prison was interesting, however, not as impacting as attending the service. The prisoners who attended the service showed a love for Jesus and Pastor Scott. The fact Scott had a similar experience in prison spoke volumes to the attendees. It was obvious they respected the message Scott shared and the compassion he expressed. After the service, many of them came up

to me thanking me for Scott and his care for them. They blessed me enormously. Thank you, Scott, for allowing me to attend this service with you. It is one of the highlights of my life. More importantly, your care for the prisoners spoke volumes to all who attended."

Questions for Discussion

1. What are some of the moments of your life that you would consider historical markers?

2. Steven Curtis Chapman wrote about remembering your chains. How do you plan on remembering the ways the Lord has freed you from your past bondage?

3. Have you ever experienced a 'desert time?' What got you through it?

4. In Scripture, wandering in the wilderness symbolizes the consequences of disobedience. Can you look back and see times where Christ was with you, even in your sinful state?

5. On the list Scott provided about the benefits of heaven, what are you looking forward to the most?

6. In what ways will the Lord use your past to lend you credibility to those whom you minister?

7. How have you seen the Holy Spirit work powerfully through you?

Finish Strong

"I have fought the good fight, I have finished the race,
I have kept the faith."
2 Timothy 4:7

"You only lose if you quit!"
Pete Lundin

A few summers ago, we hosted Vacation Bible School at our church. The theme that year was "An Amazing Desert Journey with Jesus." The kids sang songs about how fun this adventurous journey would be. The decorations were festive, showing rolling sand dunes and an oasis. The kids reenacted the journey to music as they pretended to ride on invisible camels.

For anyone who has been on a desert journey, fun is probably not the word they would use to describe it. This absence of fun was especially true of the Israelites upon whom the writers based the curriculum. They experienced the fear of attack from the Pharaoh and surrounding nations. They were hungry and thirsty, and when they found water, it was poisonous. There was much unrest and grumbling among the people, which resulted in rebellious uprisings. To make matters worse, they were traveling to a land that none of them had ever seen.

If I wanted to take an amazing journey with Jesus, I might have picked:

- A Caribbean cruise with Jesus;
- A European tour with Jesus; or
- A trip to Yosemite with Jesus.

But the people at Concordia, the curriculum publishers, got it right when they described this journey of our lives as going through the wilderness. The author of the book of Hebrews compares the Christian life to a desert journey in Hebrews 3:12-19.

> "Take care, brothers, lest there be in any of you an evil, unbelieving heart, leading you to fall away from the living God. But exhort one another every day, as long as it is called 'today,' that none of you may be hardened by the deceitfulness of sin. For we have come to share in Christ if indeed we hold our original confidence firm to the end. As it is said, 'Today, if you hear his voice, do not harden your hearts as in the rebellion.'
>
> For who were those who heard and yet rebelled? Was it not all those who left Egypt led by Moses? And with whom was he provoked for forty years? Was it not with those who sinned, whose bodies fell in the wilderness? And to whom did he swear they would not enter his rest, but to those who were disobedient? So we see that they were unable to enter because of unbelief."

God is concerned about his people finishing life's journey, unlike the Israelites, who failed to enter the Promised Land. When you get out of prison, you will face many challenges in the first couple of years as you adjust to life on the outside. Your initial reentry is only the beginning. Life is long, and it takes great perseverance to see it to its successful completion. The Hebrews passage above gives us four pointers that will help us see our voyage to its end.

Examine Yourselves

As you age, you will begin to discover strange new lumps, bumps, and pains in your body. You'll be rubbing your head and feel something odd you didn't feel before. Or maybe you will be examining your face in the morning and discover a new blemish that doesn't look quite right. *Is that skin cancer?* This examination is what we are encouraged to do regarding our hearts.

In verse 12, there is first a call to the believer to take a good look at his own heart to see if unbelief has crept into it, causing it to become evil. We all have doubts and difficulty fully trusting the Lord. The way we deal with those areas is by taking each thought captive to the obedience of Christ (see 2 Corinthians 10:5). When we discover a spot on our skin that we may think is cancer, the smart thing to do is to get to the dermatologist and take care of it while it is still treatable. Ignoring it is like turning up the radio when we hear something making noise in our engine, hoping that it will go away.

The people of Israel didn't nip their disbelief in the bud. Instead, they grumbled and complained, and soon a spirit of rebellion swept over the entire camp. When it came time for them to enter the Promised Land, they feared the giants instead of remembering the miraculous deeds the Lord had done in their midst. They fell away from the living God and transitioned from objects of God's grace to objects of his wrath.

Squash that disbelief before it takes hold in your heart. For me, this disbelief tries to come in the form of an intellectual argument. I read something in the Bible that just doesn't make sense. Then the devil whispers, "You are a fool if you believe this stuff." That is when I need to tell the devil, "I choose to have faith and not trust in my limited intellect."

Encourage One Another

One of the greatest challenges companies face when the economy tanks is keeping the employees' morale from sinking. A sense of hopelessness can make a significant impact on productivity. People tend not to work as hard when they are not sure if they will have a job, house, or family in the near future. There are dozens, if not hundreds, of sites online giving companies advice on how to keep up employee morale.

But God has the solution for us in Hebrews 3:13. He says to exhort one another every day. My wife, Mary, is very good at this. She has a network of moms with whom she talks to regularly, and they encourage one another in the difficult task of raising children and homeschooling. Some days, Mary is having a down day and needs to be lifted, and other days she is the one doing the lifting.

> She has a network of moms with whom she talks to regularly.

Life in the desert sucks the life right out of us. The world and the media are very good at discouraging us. We can become depressed when we see the condition of our country's morals. We can get discouraged when we see the economic forecast. Besides, we can become disheartened when we see all the people we have been praying for continue to turn away from God. That is why the writer of Hebrews says we need to encourage one another while it is called today. If you wonder when you should encourage your brothers and sisters, check your calendar, and if it's a day called today go for it. This encouragement is not a happy-go-lucky variety. We don't just slap a smile on and tell people everything is going to be okay. Some things may not be okay, but that doesn't change the fact that God is still for us and he will use all these things for His glory.

The best way to encourage others is by quoting the promises in the Bible. There is plenty of pop psychology on the daily TV talk shows, but it is the very words of God that we need to hear. When I go to visit the sick, they don't want to spend the entire time hearing about my life. They want to know what God thinks about their situation.

Hold onto Your Confidence

Confidence and hope are closely related. Each has to do with being sure of the things you believe. One of the main tactics the devil uses to get us off track in our Christian walk is to cause us to begin to question those things we are confident in, especially the goodness of God. The confidence the Israelites had when they left Egypt was tested when things didn't seem to be going according to plan. In Exodus 14:11, they began to challenge Moses saying, "Take us back to Egypt! Has God brought us out here in the desert just to kill us? Were there not enough graves in Egypt?" Ultimately, they were saying, "We don't believe you have our best interest in mind, God."

When you get out of prison, many things are not going to go the way you planned, and you may desire to "return to Egypt."

That old sin begins to look more tantalizing than the obedience that is right in front of you. Remember when Jesus began to say many hard things to the crowds many of them quit following him. He turned to His disciples and asked them if they were leaving too. Peter said something I find myself often saying: "Where shall we go? Only you have the words of eternal life."

The Israelites had lost confidence in God. They thought they knew what was best, not remembering the terrible life they'd escaped. Many times, when Satan tempts me to return to old, sinful habits, if I sit for a moment and remember the result of those choices, I realize I need to stay right where I am.

Tenderize Your Heart

We ate a lot of venison steak when I was a kid. The problem with deer meat is it is so lean and tough that it dries out quickly when cooked unless it is tenderized. We would take a metal mallet with spikes and pound out the meat into a thin slab so it could receive the seasoning and cook quickly.

I wish it were as easy to tenderize our hearts because a hard heart will cause you to give up the journey quicker than anything. That is why it is mentioned in two places in Hebrews 3. In verse 13, it says we become hardened by the deceitfulness of sin, and in verse 15, we see hardness leads to rebellion.

So, the question is how do we tenderize our hearts against sin and rebellion? Scripture gives us a few ways we can remain tender on our journey.

1. Be generous and giving towards our poor brothers and sisters. "If among you, one of your brothers should become poor, in any of your towns within your land that the LORD your God is giving you, you shall not

harden your heart or shut your hand against your poor brother." (Deuteronomy 15:7);

2. Obey God quickly when he convicts you of your sin. "Why should you harden your hearts as the Egyptians and Pharaoh hardened their hearts? After he had dealt severely with them, did they not send the people away, and they departed?" (1 Samuel 6:6); and

3. Ask the Lord for a new heart that is led by the Spirit. "And I will give you a new heart and a new spirit I will put within you. And I will remove the heart of stone from your flesh and give you a heart of flesh." (Ezekiel 36:26)

The Poor Example Set by Saul

In 2 Timothy 2:20–21, the Apostle Paul observes:

> "Now in a great house there are not only vessels of gold and silver but also of wood and clay, some for honorable use, some for dishonorable. Therefore, if anyone cleanses himself from what is dishonorable, he will be a vessel for honorable use, set apart as holy, useful to the master of the house, ready for every good work."

Some vessels in the house are used for more desirable purposes than others. Would you rather be a crystal flower vase or a garbage pail? In your past life, you filled your "vessel" with dishonorable things. Now, as a Christian, I hope you desire to be a vessel set aside for noble use.

In the Old Testament, we see a man who God used for honorable purposes at the beginning, but because he did not continue to cleanse himself, he ended up in a dishonorable state.

Sometimes the Scriptures show us how not to do something as a warning. Consider three ways Saul failed to finish strong.

Saul started honorably by serving his father but then dishonored himself with selfishness.

We see in 1 Samuel 9 that Saul has been out looking for his father's donkeys. As livestock are prone to do, these have wandered off. I want you to note the extent that Saul goes to in trying to find these animals. They pass through five different lands in their search. In my estimate, according to the Bible Atlas, they probably walked about 30 miles while looking for these wandering animals. But during this time, Saul was not deterred because he has one purpose in mind; to complete the mission that his father has given him.

Unfortunately, this level of honor did not carry over into his reign as king. He did not honor God the Father, as he should have. If he had shown the same kind of zeal in carrying out God's commandments that he did in finding his father's donkeys, he may have continued as the vessel of honor that the Lord could use to carry out His plans for Israel.

Samuel gave Saul instructions from the Lord to attack and annihilate the Amalekites. Saul does defeat them, but when it comes time to wipe them out completely, he does not follow the Lord's strict command but spares their king, Agag, as well as the best of the sheep, cattle, and oxen. In his heart, he second-guessed the Lord and let the people pressure him into disobedience.

> **He doubted the Lord and let people pressure him.**

When Samuel confronted him, he stated the animals were to be a sacrifice to the Lord. Samuel's response applies to us today as much as it did to

GET OUT FOR GOOD

Saul. "Behold, to obey is better than sacrifice, and to listen than the fat of rams."

Perhaps you have sacrificed much in your life for the Lord. You have given vast amounts of money and have dedicated time to the church and its work of reaching the lost with the Gospel. But all the while, there has been an area of disobedience in your life. You may even try to convince yourself it is not a big deal to God and think it is something you will sacrifice to the Lord later on.

That small disobedience may be keeping you from finishing strong as an honorable vessel for the Lord's work. You may very well be saved and trusting in Jesus, but your life here on earth has been marked by frustrating failure and a definite lack of purpose. The great news is that you can be as holy as you want to be. The Lord wants to cleanse you thoroughly! The only thing that stands in his way is you (and me).

Right after this incident, the Lord rejects Saul as king. Now, you would think he would be removed immediately from that position, but he continues to reign for over three decades. This story teaches us that sometimes a person can give the impression that God is using them, but they have been rejected. Don't let status, appearances, or titles deceive you into thinking God is cool with your area of disobedience.

Saul started honorably by not thinking too highly of himself but then dishonored himself by presuming he could offer the sacrifice.

When Samuel first approached Saul to tell him he was God's choice to be king, he was shocked. He did not consider himself worthy of consideration as the leader of God's people. Listen to Saul's reaction in 1 Samuel 9:21. "Am I not a Benjaminite, from the least of the tribes of Israel? And is not my clan the humblest of all the clans of the tribe of Benjamin? Why then have you spoken to me in this way?"

This response showed Saul's humility. Romans 12:3 tells us not to think of ourselves more highly than we should. Instead of exalting ourselves, we should wait for the Lord to promote us. This is precisely what happened to Saul. God exalted him to the highest earthly position possible. If only Saul had stayed this humble, he could have remained as an honorable vessel for the Lord's use. Instead, his pride and fear of man hindered him and knocked him out of the running.

A few chapters later, Saul was waiting around for Samuel to come and offer the daily sacrifice. This was supposed to be Saul's big moment in front of the people. When Samuel was running late, and folks began to get restless, he decides to offer the sacrifice himself.

Have you ever done anything like this—jumped ahead of the Lord? You want something so badly that you begin to wonder if the Lord has forgotten you, and you need to take things into your own hands. Saul jumped ahead of the Lord and paid dearly. When the prophet arrives, he tells him, "You have done foolishly. You have not kept the command of the LORD your God, with which he commanded you. For then, the LORD would have established your kingdom over Israel forever." This verse is challenging because I know there have been times I have jumped ahead of the Lord. Is there an instance that comes to mind in your life? Maybe it was a career choice or a relationship that didn't go the way it should have, and if you had waited on the Lord it might have turned out differently.

Remember these stories are here in the Old Testament as a warning to us so we do not fall into the same traps as they did. They are not to discourage us but to help us. Saul is dead, and his story has been written. You still have time in your life to ask the Lord to cleanse you from your false motives so you can be used for honorable service in His house and finish strong.

Saul started honorably by controlling his temper but then dishonored himself by trying to destroy all who threatened him.

One of the greatest problems in leadership is that, as time goes on, the leader begins to disregard council and becomes blind to his or her stubbornness. The reason this so quickly happens is the leader, especially those with absolute power, can crush anyone underneath them that disagrees. Soon, no one will even dare to rise and confront them because they fear what will happen. People begin only to tell the leader what they want to hear. As Lord John Acton said, "Power tends to corrupt, and absolute power corrupts absolutely. Great men are usually all bad men."

This slippery slope of corruption happened in Saul's case. He starts out fine, showing great patience when some rebellious guys question the Lord's choice in 1 Samuel 10:27. "But some worthless fellows said, 'How can this man save us?' And they despised him and brought him no present. But he held his peace."

Saul does a very wise thing; he holds his peace and lets events unfold as they will. Unfortunately, as he gained power, this habit did not continue into his later reign. He became a very suspicious and jealous man, and for good reason. He realized the kingdom had been taken from his family's line and given to David's line. Instead of accepting the Lord's judgment for his unrighteous acts, Saul lashes out in anger against David by trying to kill him with a spear.

Sometimes I am shocked at my propensity towards this kind of reaction. It comes straight from the devil. He was cast down from his heavenly position because of his pride and desire to rise in power to God's level. He did not want to remain humble and now is eternally shamed. He wants all of God's image-bearers to follow in his destructive footsteps.

What is the antidote for this kind of pride and jealousy in leadership? I find the most humbling thing we can do as leaders, whether it is in our homes, businesses, or ministries, is to admit we were wrong and then apologize to those who were affected by our stubbornness. This act cleanses the vessel! If we refuse, we become stained. We have coffee cups at home we didn't rinse out right away, and now they are forever stained! How much more so are our souls when we don't confess our sins to God and others?

The main issue is if you want to be a clean vessel for honorable use in the Lord's house or not. Dr. Don Davis, founder of The Urban Ministry Institute, told a group of prisoners, "You can be as holy as you want to be." Holiness comes at a price. That price is denying yourself, taking up your cross, and following the Lord. This decision is difficult when we forget the Lord's benefits as Saul did.

Tips for Family and Friends

Tip #1 – Life is a marathon, not a sprint. Help your loved one plan for the long haul.

When a prisoner is released from incarceration, they can be idealistic about the simplicity of transition. They think, I won't be a statistic. Others may give up, but I'm going to make it look easy. Like a runner in a 100-yard dash they take off from the starting line with a burst of speed and energy. Then, they begin to encounter obstacles along the way. When they face these hurdles, your job is to encourage them not to quit. Remind them life is long, and even though a marathon runner may slow to a crawl during the race, as long as they are moving forward they are making progress. Paul said in 2 Timothy 4:7, "I have fought the good fight, I have finished the race, I have kept the faith." The goal is finishing, not being the first to cross the finish line.

Tip #2 – When an ex-offender faces tough times and peer pressure, remind them of the Lord's many benefits.

One of the greatest challenges your loved one will face is addiction. In the past, addictions like alcohol, drugs, and sex have helped them survive and deal with their dysfunction. When they enter times of dryness, they may be tempted to return to captivity. They will begin to long for the comfort their addictions brought them. During those trying moments, don't hound them about how detrimental these cravings are. Instead, remind them of all the ways the Lord has blessed them.

Encourage them to keep running. The best strategy the prodigal son can implement is recalling the season of life when he desired the pig slop because he was so hungry. Psalm 103:2 says, "Bless the Lord, O my soul, and forget not all his benefits." During his darkest moments, David reminded his soul to thank the Lord for all the mighty deeds he had accomplished by the power of the Spirit.

Questions for Discussion

1. What are some of the challenges a person faces traveling in the desert? How do those relate to the desert journey we are on with the Lord?

2. What are some of the main hindrances to someone finishing strong?

3. Think about your addictions for a moment. Why did you love them so much? How did they help you get through difficult times?

4. Why are addictions so harmful?

5. What strategies do you plan to implement to overcome the desire to return to addictive patterns?

6. Looking at King Saul's life, what were some of his greatest mistakes?

7. Make a list of the benefits you've seen in your life since you've become a Christian.

Afterword

The main focus of this book is to provide practical, biblical steps you can take if you want to stay out of prison successfully. I know that by following these guidelines, I have decreased my chances of reoffending. But what if you follow all the advice in this book and things don't go well for you? What if you can't find a job? What if your desire for a godly spouse is met with the silence of heaven? What if you get sick or a loved one dies? All the practical advice in the world will not guarantee victory.

Job was a righteous man. He had great wealth and numerous children. Life was going according to plan. Then one day, things began to change. He lost his property, his children, and his health in a very short period. His wife even tells him, "Curse God and die. Why are you still holding on to your integrity?" Job responds, "You speak as a foolish woman. Should we accept from God only good and not adversity?" (Job 2:9). Later, he declares before his friends, "Though he slay me, yet will I trust in him: but I will maintain mine own ways before him" (Job 13:15).

To be truly successful as a disciple of Christ, you need to determine in your heart that no matter how good or bad things are, you will still cling to the Lord. If you think you're not going back to prison because you have everything in order, what happens when the rug gets pulled out from under you? You can't control your circumstances, only how you react to them. Today, declare your desire to remain faithful with the words of the old hymn attributed to an Indian prince.

> I have decided to follow Jesus
> I have decided to follow Jesus
> I have decided to follow Jesus
> No turning back no turning back
>
> The world behind me the cross before me
> The world behind me the cross before me
> The world behind me the cross before me
> No turning back no turning back
>
> Though none go with me, still I will follow
> Though none go with me, still I will follow
> Though none go with me, still I will follow
> No turning back no turning back.

Endnotes

[i] Sentencingproject.org. (2020). https://www.sentencingproject.org/wp-content/uploads/2017/05/Still-Life.pdf

[ii] Daily Kos. (2020). *75% US Recidivism Rate within 5 yrs. Could Investing a Fraction of Future Cost Lower that Number?*. [online] Available at: https://www.dailykos.com/stories/2017/12/20/1726312/-75-US-Recidivism-Rate-within-5-yrs-Could-Investing-a-Fraction-of-Future-Cost-Lower-that-Number

[iii] Lopes, Marina. (2017) *One Way Out*. [online] Available at https://www.washingtonpost.com/world/the_americas/one-way-out-pastors-in-brazil-converting-gang-members-on-youtube/2019/05/17/bc560746-614c-11e9-bf24-db4b9fb62aa2_story.html

[iv] Kiyosaki, R., Lechter, S. and Davidson, R. (2001). Rich dad, poor dad. Prince Frederick, Md.: Recorded Books.

[vi] Group, S. (2020). *3 people arrested in Sunday church robbery*. [online] KATV. Available at: https://katv.com/archive/3-people-arrested-in-sunday-church-robbery [Accessed 9 Jan. 2020].

[vii] "Breaking Away from the Flock: Sheep Do Not Behave like Sheep, Researchers Reveal." *Daily Mail Online*, Associated Newspapers, 23 July 2012, www.dailymail.co.uk/sciencetech/article-2177762/Breaking-away-flock-Sheep-behave-like-sheep-researchers-reveal.html.

[viii] "Jim Jones." *Wikipedia*, Wikimedia Foundation, 20 Jan. 2020, en.wikipedia.org/wiki/Jim_Jones.

[ix] Barclay, W. (1999). *Parables of Jesus*. Louisville: Presbyterian Publishing Corporation.

[x] Brown, H. Jackson. *Lifes Little Instruction Book*. Rutledge Hill Press, 1991.

[xi] Thoennes, Erik K., "Created to Play: Thoughts on Play Sport and the Christian Life" chapter in *The Image of God in the Human Body: Essays on Christianity and Sports*, Donald Deardorff and John White eds., Edwin Mellen Press, 2008.

[xii] Stine, David, *The Whole Life*. Howard Books, 2019.

[xiii] En.wikipedia.org. (2020). *Australia*. [online] Available at: https://en.wikipedia.org/wiki/Australia [Accessed 9 Jan. 2020].

[xiv] *ABC News* (25 July 2007). "Online records highlight Australia's convict past", Retrieved 21 September 2016.

[xv] Ers.usda.gov. (2020). [online] Available at: https://www.ers.usda.gov/webdocs/publications/47116/51556_sb968b.pdf?v=0 [Accessed 9 Jan. 2020].

[xvi] Loc.gov. (2020). *Born in Slavery: Slave Narratives from the Federal Writers' Project - Collection Connections | Teacher Resources - Library of Congress*. [online] Available at: http://www.loc.gov/teachers/classroommaterials/connections/narratives-slavery/file.html [Accessed 9 Jan. 2020].

[xvii] Harney, K. (2009). *Organic outreach for ordinary people*. Grand Rapids, Michigan: Zondervan.

Appendix A

Nicene Creed with Scripture References

We believe in one God, (Exodus 20.2-3, Mark 12.29-31) ***the Father Almighty,*** (Ephesians 4.6, Malachi 2.10, Genesis 35.11) ***Maker of heaven and earth,*** (Genesis 1.1, Isaiah 44:24) ***and of all things visible and invisible*** (Colossians 1:16, Romans 1:20).

And in one Lord Jesus Christ, (2 Corinthians 1:3, I Thessalonians 1:1, Romans 13:14) ***the only-begotten Son of God, begotten of the Father before all worlds;*** (John 3:16, Hebrews 1:6, Matthew 14:33, Revelation 1:8) ***God of God, Light of Light, true God of true God; begotten, not made,*** (John 1:1, I John 1:5, John 8:12, John 20:28, I John 5:20, Psalms 2:7, Hebrews 1:5, John 14:9) ***being of one substance with the Father;*** (John 10:30, Isaiah 44:6, Revelation 1:8, Philippians 2:6, John 10:38, Colossians 2:9) ***by whom all things were made*** (John 1:1-3,10,14, I Corinthians 8:6, Colossians 1:15-17).

Who, for us, and for our salvation, came down from heaven, (I Thessalonians 5:9, Acts 4:12, II Timothy 3:15, John 6:51, John 6:38, Matthew 1:18, Luke 1:27,35, Philippians 2:6,7 , Romans 1:3) ***and was incarnate by the Holy Spirit of the virgin Mary,*** (Matthew 1:18, Luke 1:27, 35) ***and was made man;*** (Philippians 2:6-7, Romans 1:3) ***and was crucified also for us under Pontius Pilate*** (Acts 2:36, Matthew 27:2,26, Mark 15:15). ***He suffered and was buried; and the third day He rose again, in accordance with the Scriptures;*** (Matthew 16:21, Mark 15:46, Luke 24:5-7, I Corinthians 15:3-4) ***and ascended into heaven, and sits at the right hand of the Father;*** (John 20:17, I Timothy 3:16, I Peter 3:21,22, Acts 1:9, Mark 16:19) ***and He shall come again, with glory, to judge the living and the***

dead; whose kingdom shall have no end (Acts 1:10,11, Revelation 1:7, John 5:22, Acts 10:42, Luke 1:33).

And I believe in the Holy Spirit, the Lord and Giver of Life; (John 14:17, II Corinthians 3:17, Acts 5:3,4, John 3:5, Titus 3:5) *who proceeds from the Father and the Son; who with the Father and the Son together is worshipped and glorified; who spoke by the prophets* (John 15:26, Luke 11:13, Matthew 28:19, II Peter 1:21).

And I believe in one holy universal and apostolic Church (John 17:20-23, Ephesians 4:1-6, Colossians 1:18, Hebrews 12:23, Revelation 21:27, Philippians 4:3, Matthew 18:20, Philemon 1:2, Romans 16:5, I Timothy 3:15, Ephesians 2:20, Acts 2:42). *I acknowledge one baptism for the remission of sins* (Matthew 28:18,19, Ephesians 4:5, Galatians 3:27, Matthew 26:28, Luke 24;47, Acts 2:38, I Peter 3:21, Romans 6:3,4) *and I look for the resurrection of the dead, and the life of the world to come* (1 Corinthians 15:12, 1 Corinthians 15:21,22, John 3:16, 1 Corinthians 2:9, -Romans 11:36). ***Amen***

About the Author

Scott Stroud was born and raised in Minnesota and Wisconsin. Due to an unstable family life, he moved twenty-seven times as a child. Early on he became involved with theft and drinking leading to an armed robbery in 1991, resulting in a four-year prison sentence. He became a Christian during his time there and upon his release began to minister to those still in prison.

He was a barber for 20 years, owning a shop in North Minneapolis for 12 years. He currently serves as a pastor in Salinas, California, with his beautiful wife, Mary, and their four terrific children. In his free time, he loves to bake pies, play golf, and sample new restaurants with his family.

If you would like to contact Scott about speaking at your church or prison ministry event, contact him at sixstrouds@gmail.com.

Coming Soon!

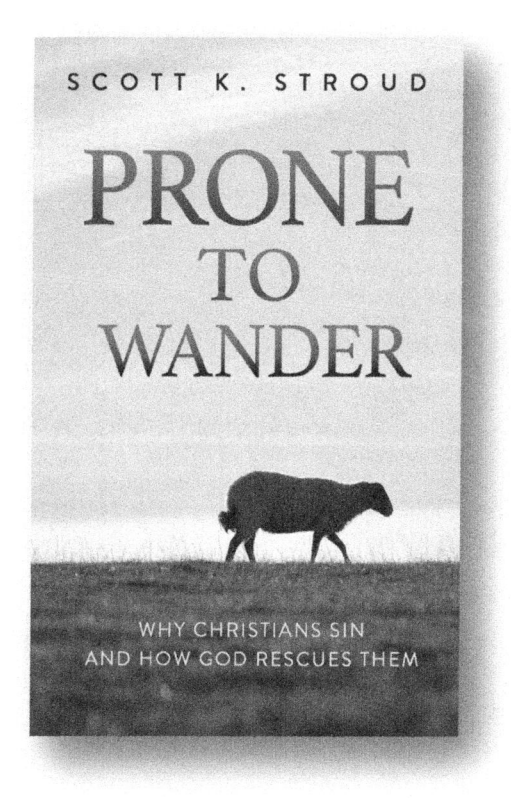

Christians have been baffled by the problem of sin for millennia. Questions like, *'Why can't I seem to overcome this issue?'* and *'Why do some people seem to easily live righteous lives while I struggle?'* continue to confound the faithful.

In his new book, *Prone to Wander,* Scott K. Stroud points to patterns in the lives of sheep to address these questions. Release set for fall of 2020. For more information visit www.scottkstroud.com